MICHIGAN'S HAUNTED LIGHTHOUSES

MICHIGAN'S HAUNTED LIGHTHOUSES

DIANNA HIGGS STAMPFLER

HAUNTED
AMERICA

Published by Haunted America
A Division of The History Press
Charleston, SC
www.historypress.com

Front cover: Saginaw River Rear Range Lighthouse by Mike Sonneberg. *LostInMichigan.net.*

First published 2019

Manufactured in the United States

ISBN 9781467141994

Library of Congress Control Number: 2018963520

*Dedicated to all the passionate keepers of Michigan's lighthouses
and those who refuse to let their histories be extinguished*

MICHIGAN'S
HAUNTED LIGHTHOUSES

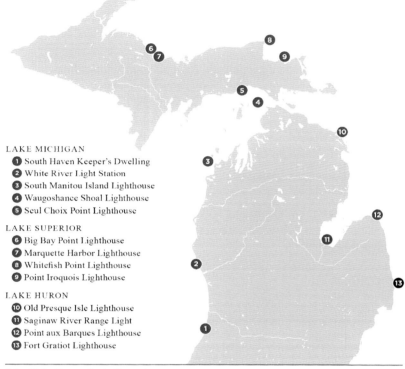

LAKE MICHIGAN
1. South Haven Keeper's Dwelling
2. White River Light Station
3. South Manitou Island Lighthouse
4. Waugoshance Shoal Lighthouse
5. Seul Choix Point Lighthouse

LAKE SUPERIOR
6. Big Bay Point Lighthouse
7. Marquette Harbor Lighthouse
8. Whitefish Point Lighthouse
9. Point Iroquois Lighthouse

LAKE HURON
10. Old Presque Isle Lighthouse
11. Saginaw River Range Light
12. Point aux Barques Lighthouse
13. Fort Gratiot Lighthouse

Other Lights Rumored to be Haunted

LAKE MICHIGAN	LAKE SUPERIOR	LAKE HURON
Beaver Head Island Lighthouse	Copper Harbor Lighthouse	New Presque Isle Lighthouse
Peninsula Point Lighthouse	Crisp Point Lighthouse	Pipe Island Lighthouse
Sand Point Lighthouse	Eagle Harbor Lighthouse	Sturgeon Point Lighthouse
Squaw Island Lighthouse	Fourteen Mile Point Lighthouse	Thunder Bay Island Lighthouse
St. Joseph Keeper's Residence	Grand Island Lighthouse	
St. Helena Island Lighthouse	Ontonagon Lighthouse	
	Rock of Ages Lighthouse	
	Rock Harbor Lighthouse	
	Stannard Rock Lighthouse	

This list may not include all Michigan lights that are rumored to be haunted. Some have been left off at the request of the owners or managing organizations. If you have others to add to the list, including stories and photos, please email Travel@PromoteMichigan.com.

The numbers on this map of Michigan lighthouses correspond to the chapters.
Author's Collection.

CONTENTS

PREFACE

I was in the dark about Michigan's historic lighthouses until 1997, when I began working at the West Michigan Tourist Association (WMTA)—the oldest continually operating regional tourist association in the country. My first project as the marketing and media director was to research the lights on the official 1,100-mile Lake Michigan Circle Tour (LMCT) route, established in 1987 by Jack Morgan of the Michigan Department of Transportation.

I'm not sure how I made it through my life up until that point having no concept of lighthouses and the fact that Michigan has more than any other state, but that was a turning point for me. The lighthouses, and more importantly the stories of their keepers, became an immediate (and ongoing) fascination for me.

While at WMTA, I took the information I had gathered for the *Lake Michigan Circle Tour Map & Guide* and created a lighthouse presentation that I could share with groups at senior centers, libraries, museums, civic clubs and schools. Back in those days, it was a carousel slide show versus today's PowerPoint presentation.

I left WMTA in 2004 to launch my own consulting company, called Promote Michigan, offering services in public relations, social media, event planning and promotion around the state. I'm a freelance writer and broadcaster, and I'm still sharing "Michigan's Haunted Lighthouses" (previously known as "Michigan's Ghostly Beacons") and "Ladies of the Lights" on a regular basis. I'm excited that I now also have a book, with my name on the cover, to serve as a companion to the program.

Over the years, I've held memberships in the Historical Society of Michigan and the Great Lakes Lighthouse Keepers Association—both have been instrumental in fueling my continued love of my home state of Michigan as well as my passion for lighthouses. Since I began working on this book, I've also felt compelled to join many of the other lighthouse and maritime associations around the state—because without these organizations, I wouldn't have had access to much of the information, documents and images that you find here.

Three individuals stand out for their early inspiration and support of me as a novice lighthouse historian:

Dick Moehl, who I met back in my WMTA days when he was the president of the Great Lakes Lighthouse Keepers Association (GLLKA). Dick passed away in late 2015, but I'll always remember him for his dedication to our state's historic lights.

Terry Pepper, who currently serves as the GLLKA president and maintains what I consider to be the premier website about Great Lakes lighthouses at TerryPepper.com. Whenever I need to verify information or clarify some fact or another, Terry and his website are there. Whenever someone asks me for information, I send them to Terry's site first, because chances are if he doesn't have it, no one else does either.

Fred Stonehouse, a well-known author and historian, whose countless books have provided information, entertainment and motivation for me in writing this book. I am honored to be able to quote all three of these legendary men as solid sources of places, names and dates for Michigan's many haunted lighthouses throughout the pages of this book.

This project has been one filled with passion and excitement on a multitude of levels. It's allowed me to revisit many of our lights, gather more ghostly stories and work with my dad to research the family histories of these keepers. I hope you enjoy reading it as much as I did writing it! And thank you to my dear friend and "personal editor" Paula, who took time out of her summer vacation to proofread this manuscript.

Acknowledgements

T hank you to my parents, who instilled in me a love of history, travel and storytelling; my children, who continue to indulge me in my passion for all things Michigan; and my favorite traveling companion, ghost hunter and tombstone tourist.

INTRODUCTION

M ichigan doesn't have an official state structure, but if it did, it would likely be either the 5-mile Mackinac Bridge (opened in 1957 and an aid to navigation itself) or a lighthouse to represent the 120 or so beacons that stand tall along more than 3,200 miles of Great Lakes freshwater shoreline.

Well before Michigan became the twenty-sixth state in the Union on January 26, 1837, lighthouses were becoming a recognized part of the landscape, serving as navigational aids for shipping, fishing, lumbering and mining industries that shaped the state's early history.

The first was Fort Gratiot, constructed at the entrance of the St. Clair River and Lake Huron in 1825 by Lucius Lyon—a pioneer, surveyor and eventual deputy surveyor general of the Michigan Territory. He later represented Michigan in the U.S. House of Representatives and U.S. Senate. Named after General Charles Gratiot, who engineered the construction of the nearby Fort Gratiot Military Outpost in 1814, this was one of the few European settlements north of Detroit at the time.

The city of St. Joseph was home to the first light station on Lake Michigan, dating back to 1832 (although the current range light system wasn't built until 1906–1907). That first lighthouse was a single-story dwelling made of stone. In 1859, a new, two-story structure was built on a bluff overlooking the city. It remained operational until 1924 and was demolished in 1955. During the early years, St. Joseph also was home to the lighthouse depot for Lake Michigan until service was transferred to Milwaukee in 1917.

Construction began in 1847 on the Whitefish Point Light Station on Lake Superior, regarded as the most important beacon on that body of water as all vessels entering and leaving the lake must pass by. It was near Whitefish Point, in 1975, that the *Edmund Fitzgerald* sank on November 10 during an early-season squall. It is no wonder this treacherous shoreline of Lake Superior is known as the "Graveyard of the Great Lakes," as there are more shipwrecks here than any other locale on the lake.

On a national level, all lighthouses were administered by the U.S. Treasury's Lighthouse Establishment, which was formed in 1791. After great dissatisfaction with the administration of these lights, responsibility for them was removed from the Treasury Department by an act of Congress in 1853 and transferred to the U.S. Lighthouse Board, which became the second agency of the federal government to take over responsibility for the construction and maintenance of all lights and other navigation aids. Around 1910, it fell to the Lighthouse Service, under the Department of Commerce, to maintain these maritime structures. The Lighthouse Service merged with the U.S. Coast Guard in 1939.

Serving as a lighthouse keeper in the mid- to late 1800s and into the early twentieth century was a government position often hired by the office of the president of the United States. During the Civil War and in the years that followed, many veterans found work serving as keepers, including Captain James S. Donahue in South Haven and Aaron Sheridan on South Manitou Island. Despite both men being wounded in battle with what many would consider debilitating injuries (Donahue lost a leg and Sheridan lost the use of an arm), these heroic keepers were diligent in their duties of tending to their respective lights and also assisted with lifesaving duties as needed.

Tending a lighthouse wasn't a job one took lightly. Most of the keepers who accepted the challenging role did so with a great sense of pride and dedication—like Captain William Robinson at White River Light Station in Whitehall. He was instrumental in the construction of the light, and he was named its first official keeper in 1875—a position he held for forty-four years before passing away at the light in 1919 at the age of eighty-seven.

For others, lighthouse keeping was a family business with duties shared among husbands and wives, children and grandchildren, uncles and nephews, brothers and sisters. This was the case with Julia Tobey Brawn Way in Saginaw, who served as keeper when her husband, Peter, became disabled and was unable to tend to the light. She ended up outliving two husband keepers and working alongside her son, Dewitt.

Many question why so many of Michigan's lighthouses are rumored to be haunted, and questions arise as to who these spirits really are. Nearly one-fifth of all the lights in the state, past and present, have a ghostly story to be told.

Maybe it is the tragic deaths that occurred during those early days when ships sank and keepers risked or lost their lives in the line of duty that creates these unsettled souls. Such is the case at Big Bay Point Lighthouse, northwest of Marquette, where a distraught William Prior took his own life after his son died from an injury sustained while tending the light.

And it can be expected that local lore has something to do with the legends that are passed on from generation to generation, growing like tall tales, something akin to fake news in today's world of digital media.

Dick Moehl once told me something to the effect that "every lighthouse worth a grain of salt has a good ghost story, and if there isn't one, you just make one up."

Regardless of the truthfulness of the ghost stories, the histories of the lighthouses and their keepers are well documented in Michigan's past, and thanks to dedicated individuals who have worked tirelessly to preserve them, their future looks bright as well.

If you have a ghost story to share, please email Travel@PromoteMichigan.com.

LAKE MICHIGAN

1

SOUTH HAVEN KEEPER'S DWELLING

N early 150 years after he first began his service at the lighthouse in South Haven, James Samuel Donahue remains one of the town's most noted historical figures. Maybe that is because he continues to make his presence known to those who work and visit the keeper's residence where he raised his family and dedicated his life to protecting those who traveled the waters of the Black River and Lake Michigan.

Today, the residence is home to more than Donahue's ghost—it is a library and research facility operated by the Michigan Maritime Museum. Staff, researchers and volunteers have long shared accounts of mysterious goings-on inside the home, from the creaking of floorboards upstairs when no one was there to opening and closing of doors. However, the ghost is more of a presence than a nuisance. Donahue, like many of the other spirits that linger at Michigan lights, simply feels more comfortable inside the protective walls of his one-time home.

Yet not everyone who has had access to this building over the years has had the pleasure of meeting its resident spirit.

"I haven't seen any ghosts at the keeper's house. I guess I'm forewarned in any case," Kenneth Pott said in a 2000 article in the *Herald Palladium*, a St. Joseph, Michigan–based newspaper. Pott served nineteen years as a curator and archaeologist at the Michigan Maritime Museum and over the years has been active with the Michigan Museums Association Board, American Association of Museums, Historical Society of Michigan and Western Michigan University's Frederick S. Upton Fellowship Program in Public History.

James Samuel Donahue enlisted in June 1861 as a private in Company A, Eighth Michigan Infantry, fighting in several battles during the Civil War. *Michigan Maritime Museum.*

Born to Irish immigrants Manday and Nellie (Loan) Donahue on March 18, 1840, in Addison County, Vermont, James Samuel Donahue was one of seven children. At the age of twelve, he took a job on a whaling ship, sailing around the Pacific and Arctic Oceans for nearly four years before returning to the New England area. He landed in Detroit shortly thereafter and enlisted in June 1861 as a private in Company A, Eighth Michigan Infantry, fighting in the Civil War.

Donahue was active in several battles, taking a hit to his shoulder during an engagement on James Island, South Carolina. He was laid up for several weeks but returned to the front line and saw action at Cumberland Gap, Antietam and Strawberry Plains, Tennessee, among other battles.

On May 6, 1864, his left leg was struck by a conical-shaped Minié ball, resulting in an amputation at the thigh. Discharged four months later, he returned to Detroit before moving to Gratiot County (in the center of the Lower Peninsula), where he married Sophia Oberlin on June 17, 1872.

During this time, the port town of South Haven was taking shape around Michigan's thriving lumbering industry. A large sawmill was constructed in 1866 by George Hannas, followed by a series of stores, hotels, saloons and churches. Tourists came next, followed by a growing agricultural industry in an area later referred to as the "Fruit Belt" due to a lake-effect climate that provides the ideal conditions. With an influx of traffic along the area waterways, harbor improvements became increasingly important.

As the Army Corps of Engineers worked to increase the width of the channel and extend the piers, the Lighthouse Board requested an appropriation of $6,000 in 1868 for the construction of a pier-head beacon and keeper's dwelling. However, Congress later recalled unexpended funds, putting an immediate halt to the project.

Back on track by 1871, a 30-foot-tall wooden light with an octagonal cast-iron lantern was built at the end of the pier. A 75-foot-long wooden catwalk was also erected, allowing the keeper to access the light tower even when waves were crashing over the pier below. Captain W.P. Bryan was the first keeper, activating the light for the first time in 1872. Shortly thereafter, the keeper's residence was constructed on a bluff overlooking the Black River just a short 1,125-foot walk from the light.

Captain Bryan's tenure in South Haven was short lived, and he was removed from service at the end of the 1873 season. The *South Haven Sentinel* reported on his departure on November 15, 1873:

> *Capt. W.P. Bryan received notice Monday evening from the Secretary of the Treasury that his services as lighthouse keeper at this port were no longer necessary. No successor was named in the letter, neither has the Captain an intimation as to who his successor is to be. Justice to humanity demanded that there should be a light on the pier, and the Captain has attended to it through the week notwithstanding his peremptory dismissal without any known cause. The management of the light during the past season has been satisfactory to every sailor, and if the Captain was discharged on any report made, we think the Secretary should listen to the appeals of our citizens for reinstatement. We have several times been opposed to the Captain in local matters, but we have no hesitation in saying that as Director of our Union School and attending to the needs in the night time of our marine friends he has proven himself the right man in the right place.*

The following March, thirty-four-year-old, one-legged Donahue accepted the position of acting lighthouse keeper—the second of only six men to officially tend the light. He and Sophia moved to the shoreline community where, on March 17, 1875, they welcomed their only son, Edward M. Donahue. Sadly, Sophia passed away just four months later, on July 3, at the age of twenty-seven.

The captain's log book for that date includes a sad entry: "Rain and cloudy, wind moderate, lake smooth, the night dark, the weather warm—my wife died this afternoon at 4 pm, of lung disease." The following day, he wrote: "Foggy, wind, the fog thick all day, the lake smooth, the night dark—I berryed [*sic*] my wife today at 4 pm."

The following spring, on April 19, 1876, Donahue married his second wife, Anna Kyme. Over time, they expanded their family with five sons, Walter L., John Bagley, Calvin C., James M. and Watson B., and a daughter, Kathryn A. It must have been cozy quarters inside the home, given that his mother-in-law, Ann Kyme; brother-in-law, George; and George's wife, Juliette, also lived with them. The 1910 census also listed Thomas Kyme as

The keeper's residence in South Haven was always full of members of the Donahue extended family. The captain is pictured on the left with crutches. *Michigan Maritime Museum.*

a resident. But with more people comes more help in keeping up the house and tending to the light—especially given Donahue's war injuries.

It is known that Donahue walked with the assistance of crutches and later a peg leg of sorts, neither of which would have made it easy for him to make his way down to the pier or lighthouse, let alone climb the thirty-seven-and-a-half-foot tower (later extended another five or six feet in height, still relatively short by lighthouse standards). Having the assistance of family and occasionally friends or others in town would have made his job easier to manage.

"We have several photographs of him with the crutches as well as a contemporary painting (1895–1900) depicting him with crutches and no wooden leg," according to an email from Emily Stap, collections and office manager at the Michigan Maritime Museum and Marialyce Canonie Great Lakes Research Library in South Haven. "But, from his journals he mentions applying for an artificial limb."

On December 13, 1877, he noted: "I received transportation from Major G.B. Dandy to go to New York to precure [*sic*] an artificial limb," and years later, on October 19, 1885, he noted: "I was at the station all day and night with the exception of gowing [*sic*] to the bank and drawing 75.00 from the government for a leg."

The local newspaper, *South Haven Messenger*, even noted both walking aides in an 1890 article that mentions Donahue "has been encumbered with a wooden leg and crutches ever since the war."

Up until 1887, there was no lifesaving station in South Haven, which meant Donahue was also responsible for monitoring the shoreline as ships traveled in and out of the area for business and pleasure. It is said he is credited with saving fifteen lives during his years of service, including a couple of instances where his sons (Calvin and James) found themselves in distress while in the water near the pier.

Donahue's efforts never went unnoticed; residents and city officials regarded him as a local hero. On the evening of his forty-sixth birthday in 1885, he was called upon by fifty-two seamen who presented him with a gold medal engraved with an image of the South Haven lighthouse on one side and his name and date on the other.

This paired well with the silver medal he received from the federal government, inscribed on one side with "To Capt. James S. Donahue, for bravely rescuing several persons from drowning in 1875–1889."

Tending a lighthouse was a tedious and often grueling job for any man (or woman). Imagine having to carry a cast-iron pail full of hot whale oil, lard or, in Donahue's case, kerosene down the pier (or catwalk, depending on the weather conditions) then up the staircase to the lantern room each and every day (sometimes multiple times a day).

Now imagine taking on that responsibility while walking with a peg leg or on crutches, as would have been customary for Donahue. Add to that the fact that his keeper's residence was (and still is) a short walk from the tower itself. According to records, conditions warranted that Donahue spend the night inside the tower itself nearly ninety nights during his decades of service. There were even accounts of the determined captain crawling on his hands and knees along the pier with a lit lantern between his teeth to make it to the light during inclement weather. Talk about dedication to the job.

During Donahue's tenure, improvements continued at the light station. In 1890, the South Haven beacon was chosen to test a Walsbach burner gasoline light, which turned out to double the intensity of the light and reduce the consumption of fuel by half. The pier was extended in 1901, and shortly thereafter, a fifth-order Fresnel lens was installed.

A new cylindrical metal tower came next, replacing the wooden structure that had suffered thirty years of wear and tear at the hands of Lake Michigan and Mother Nature. The prefabricated steel tower arrived in October 1903 aboard the tender *Hyacinth*, with Captain E.B. Marquette at the helm. Crews worked to secure it to the pier, install the catwalk and Fresnel lens and then paint it white before Captain Donahue proudly ascended the spiral staircase for its inaugural lighting on November 13.

One would think lighthouse tending would take up all the keeper's free time, but that wasn't the case with Donahue. Registered as a Republican, he served two terms as president of the village board and was a member of the Blue Lodge Chapter and Council of the Masonic fraternity, holding several officer positions. He was also post commander of the M.J. Dickinson Post No. 345 of the Grand Army of the Republic (GAR) and a member of the Enterprise Club.

To supplement his government salary, Donahue invested in other businesses. In the mid-1880s, he started Donahue Boat Livery. He was also the first operator of the pump house in the city's waterworks building beginning in 1892. He also dabbled in real estate and is believed to have served at one point as postmaster.

In all, Donahue served more than thirty-five years as this town's lighthouse keeper, handling the day-to-day responsibilities while also being challenged with the dangerous job of rescue efforts. It was the only light he ever tended. He retired in 1909 and passed away in 1917 at the age of seventy-five. Anna died in 1934 at the age of eighty. Donahue and both his wives are buried in Lakeview Cemetery just outside of downtown South Haven.

When the lighthouse in South Haven was automated in 1940, the Lighthouse Service transferred responsibility for navigational aids to the U.S. Coast Guard, which still maintains the now-red tower, pier and catwalk. At that time, the keeper's residence was also used as crew quarters for the Coast Guard. Eventually, the home was abandoned and later assumed by the General Services Administration (GSA), an independent agency of the U.S. government established in 1949 to help manage and support the basic functioning of federal agencies.

In 1991, the Michigan Maritime Museum leased the keeper's residence from the government as a place to house its archives and other historical documents. A few years later, the government began to sell off excess properties such as lighthouses and other related structures, and that nearly happened in South Haven.

On August 3, 2000, the home and property were deeded to the city, and it is now on permanent lease by the museum as the Marialyce Canonie Great Lakes Research Library, the only institution of its kind in the state to archive and share information on the entire scope of Michigan's maritime

Captain Donahue retired in 1909 and passed away in 1917 at the age of seventy-five. He is buried in Lakeview Cemetery just outside of downtown South Haven alongside his two wives. *Author's Collection.*

history, with a collection of nearly four thousand books, videotapes, sound recordings, maps, DVDs, nautical charts, periodicals—and even a ghost.

Given that he served longer than any other keeper in South Haven—as many years as all five other keepers combined—it would make sense that the spirit that walks the floors inside the keeper's residence belongs to Captain Donahue. One might also speculate whether his first wife, Sophia, who died at the light in 1875 of lung disease, might also reside in the historic home.

Emily Stap says:

> None of the current staff have had any experiences with ghost activity at the keeper's house. We definitely understand the fascination of haunts and ghosts—after all, as historians, perhaps we are more in tune with dead people. As a reputable Museum, we strive to provide the public with facts and truths regarding the past. The stories and hearsay about Donahue have been going on since before any of the current staff members came to the Museum. Any mysterious noises are no doubt caused by the wind (the house being high on the bluff) and the creaks and groans are the natural ones that old houses make...but you can never be sure. IF Captain Donahue's spirit lingers on in the keeper's house it is because he continues to watch his light and this harbor with dignity and honor...just as he did in life.

During the summer of 2015, I was invited by the Michigan Maritime Museum to share my presentation "Michigan's Ghostly Beacons" on the lawn of the keeper's residence. Arriving with plenty of time before set-up, I asked for a personal tour of the home I'd only heard about and seen in pictures. I walked in through the kitchen door at the back of the house, through the main floor and upstairs through the former bedrooms to the archive areas. I quietly called out to Captain Donahue, hoping he would make his presence known. I stood quietly on the creaky wooden floors, waiting for a sound or a feeling that would let me know the keeper was there and welcomed me into his home. Sadly, I was not granted the privilege of such a visit.

Back in the kitchen, I asked the volunteers who were there setting up for the program if they had ever experienced anything "interesting" at the house that might be attributed to Captain Donahue, and I was pleased to hear that they had. There were stories of footsteps and doors opening on their own, of voices and unexplainable cold spots. I think most who have spent any significant time inside the home on Michigan Avenue would agree that even though Captain Donahue passed away in 1917,

The Michigan Maritime Museum operates the Marialyce Canonie Great Lakes Research Library at the former keeper's residence at 91 Michigan Avenue in South Haven. *Author's Collection.*

his presence is still an integral part of their town's history, and there's something comforting in that fact.

The South Haven pier is accessible to the public; parking is available at the adjacent city beach. The tower is not open to the public. The lighthouse is now painted red with an elevated iron catwalk. The current light shines red and extends for thirteen nautical miles.

The keeper's residence is owned by the City of South Haven and is on lease to the Michigan Maritime Museum. It is not open to the general public except with advance reservations.

MARIALYCE CANONIE GREAT LAKES RESEARCH LIBRARY
91 Michigan Avenue
South Haven, MI 49090

2

WHITE RIVER LIGHT STATION, WHITEHALL

White River Light Station has stood proudly at the mouth of the White River in Whitehall since its fourth-order Fresnel lens was first lit in the spring of 1876, a year after construction was completed—thanks to the dedication of William "Bill" Robinson III.

Bill and his wife, Sarah (Cooper) Robinson, immigrated from England to West Michigan looking for work in the 1860s with seven of their eventual thirteen children (two of whom died in early childhood). More than 150 years later, they remain two of the noted residents of this small town along the shores of Lake Michigan.

Karen McDonnell, who lived at the light from 1983 until 2012 as a modern-day keeper and museum curator, had countless encounters with the ghosts of both Bill and Sarah during her twenty-nine years there.

In a story published on April 26, 2007, on AbsoluteMichigan.com, McDonnell said she would occasionally hear footsteps on the stairway leading to the lantern room. A distinctive cadence led her to believe it was Bill, who walked in his later years with the aid of a cane.

"I like the comfort it gives me," she said at the time. "It's like a watchman, just making sure everything is okay before it's too late at night." Even when Karen was away from the light and others stepped in to help, the infamous ghost continued his nightly rounds, perhaps to the shock and concern of the temporary staff.

Karen also recounts another, more interesting spirit, that of the keeper's wife. Although she lived a relatively short life, passing away in 1891 of a stroke at the age of fifty-three, Sarah was known around town as a meticulous housekeeper and a dedicated mother. Anyone who has lived near the shoreline knows what a challenge it is to keep a house tidy during the summer months, when windows and doors are open to allow blowing sand, dust and pollen to collect on the furniture.

The story goes that one day, Karen, who herself was no stranger to the challenges of maintaining a well-kept lakefront home, went to the second level to dust before the museum opened for the day. During the course of her chores, the phone rang, and she went downstairs to answer the call (before the days of cell phones, of course).

Afterward, Karen made her way back upstairs to complete her cleaning job, only to discover someone had already finished the work—even though she was alone in the lighthouse. She had left her dusting cloth and spray on top of a dirty display case and returned to find that the dust was gone and the cleaning supplies had moved from one side of the case to the other.

Knowing Sarah's reputation and having been witness to Bill's presence previously, Karen suspected that the lighthouse keeper's wife was

The ghost of Sarah Robinson, wife of keeper William Robinson, has been reported in this second-floor bedroom. This is believed to be the room where her children once slept. *Author's Collection.*

responsible for this simple gesture of kindness. Not one to take any act lightly, Karen quietly thanked Sarah for her help and proceeded with her day.

Over the course of the next several months, a curious Karen couldn't get the housekeeping ghost out of her mind. She wondered if the visit was a one-time occurrence or if Sarah remained on along with her husband to take care of their beloved light.

During that time, Karen would try to re-create the original scenario, leaving the dusting cloth and spray at various locations around the light. To her dismay, her attempts were futile until she returned to the room of the original incident. Once again, Karen left the dusting supplies on the display and vacated the room. This time, the infamous ghost returned and cleared the case of its coating of dust.

Upon further research, Karen discovered that the room in question had been the nursery where Sarah had cared for her children. At the time of her death, Sarah's youngest child was about sixteen years old.

Not all encounters with the spirits here are wanted or even appreciated, such as the case of Phyllis from Michigan who visited White River Light Station on a beautiful, warm, sunny day in August 2015. She said via email:

> *Well, let me first say I am not a "ghost hunter," but I truly love lighthouses. My husband and I travel Michigan and have visited most of Michigan's lighthouses. On the day we visited the lighthouse, I had a highly unusual experience.*
>
> *We had been traveling down a picturesque road and I noticed a sign identifying a lighthouse. I was very excited to see it. We pulled into the parking lot and my eyes were immediately drawn to the second floor. My husband had requested I wait for him, he was locking the car, but I continued to walk to the lighthouse.*
>
> *I entered and just began walking up the stairs, focusing on the second floor. The presenter/cashier called out to me several times, which I didn't hear. He became upset stating "you have to pay to enter." Another customer touched me and said, "that gentleman wants you to pay." I was completely amazed that I had never seen him or the other people in the lobby.*
>
> *By that time my husband had entered and inquired why I would just ignore everyone else. I said, "I have to go to the second floor," and let him pay. I reached the "Captain's" library and was literally mesmerized by a portrait of a seaman.*

My husband walked in, looked around and continued to go up the spiral staircase. He claims he called to me several times, which I have no memory of. He and some other guests were amazed at the views from the top.

He came down, asked me several times why I was acting weird and non-responsive. I told him I didn't want to go up, I wanted to stay.

He literally put my hand in his and began walking up the stairs. He was in front and I began feeling a pulling on my leg. I couldn't move my legs and I explained to my husband I couldn't move. He waited and I attempted to continue up the stairs. Once I made it, I was filled with anxiety and felt I needed to go back to the library.

At that point, I ran down the steps almost feeling a push. I was back in front of that portrait and others were in the room, I couldn't speak, I felt compelled to stare at the portrait, I think I began to believe I would not be allowed to leave the eerie experience.

I dropped my eyes from the portrait and began reading aloud the titles of the books, stating out loud, I have read that book etc. It was as if I was talking to him. I then got very scared and asked another person if they had seen my husband. The woman laughed and said, "He's been calling you for a while, you ignored him." I went down the stairs now feeling I was being held and pulled backwards. I left the building and ran to the car. My husband continued to ask what was wrong.

I said to him, "I think that place is haunted." He laughed and said, "Why?" I then asked him to go in with me again and not to leave me. I approached the cashier and apologized for walking past him earlier. I then said, "Is this lighthouse haunted?"

He kinda laughed and said, "I don't know. I haven't seen anything." I then said, "Ok, let's put it this way. Did someone die in this lighthouse?" He looked at me long and hard and said, "Yes." I said, "It happened on the second floor." He replied that it was the man in the portrait.

I can honestly say I was absolutely terrified and I know in my heart that Captain is in that house. I went to the front of the property and I swear I saw him in the window. I made my husband leave and that is one lighthouse I will never visit again. The weird thing is, I continue to find postcards or pictures of that lighthouse in various places I visit when they have no reason to have them there (like restaurants or hotels).

So, what was it that brought the Robinsons all the way to Michigan from England? It is believed Bill was drawn to the area by the active lumbering industry and the prospect of a job, perhaps even captaining a schooner to haul the freshly harvested wood from the towering forests nearby to ports in Chicago or Detroit. Lumbering was one of the top industries in the region during the end of the nineteenth century given the access to hardwoods in and around the dense forests.

The 23.6-mile-long White River rises from the Oxford Swamp in what is now north central Newaygo County, flowing westward through the Manistee National Forest and into Muskegon County and White Lake before discharging into Lake Michigan near the towns of Whitehall and Montague.

LighthouseFriends.com reports that 635 ships cleared the harbor at White River in 1871 carrying over 61,000 tons of cargo—including nearly 45 million feet of lumber, over 32 million shingles and 61,600 railroad ties.

That was also the year of the great fires that not only destroyed Chicago but also affected several Michigan towns, such as Holland and Manistee on Lake Michigan and Alpena and Port Huron on Lake Huron. Rebuilding these towns ultimately took its toll on Michigan as the rich hardwood forests were cleared to provide the natural resources to reconstruct homes and businesses around the Midwest.

Maybe it was this increased volume of traffic on the White River that first prompted Bill to contact the Lighthouse Service with a request that a lighthouse be built here to guide vessels in and out of White Lake. For years, he kept logs of the river traffic, including the dates, times, ships and what they were carrying, to further document the need for a lighthouse.

He was diligent in his efforts, sending countless letters over the course of several years. And while he waited, he took it upon himself to walk the banks of the river on a nightly basis to hang a lantern—albeit a dim one—on a shepherd's hook to mark the mouth of the river.

Between 1866 and 1871, the construction of a new channel between White Lake and Lake Michigan delayed the arrival of a true lighthouse here. But a small pyramid tower was erected in 1872 for the mere cost of $1,059 ($112,000 had been spent on the channel). Bill tended to this light and was also hired to help five other local men to construct the yellow-hued cream brick building atop a Great Lakes limestone foundation. The work was completed in late 1875, but the massive yet delicate fourth-order Fresnel lens didn't arrive until the following spring.

During those years, the captains and crews of the ships that had been safely navigating in and out of the White River thanks to Bill's relentless dedication collectively petitioned the Lighthouse Service all but demanding that he be appointed the first keeper of the new lighthouse.

William Robinson III was instrumental in the construction of the White River Light Station in Whitehall and was subsequently appointed its first keeper in 1875. He served until his death at the light in 1919. *Archives of Michigan.*

On May 31, 1876, the forty-five-year-old Bill climbed the tower to illuminate the beacon for the first time. It was a task he would grow accustomed to as he served more than forty years here—and it was the only light he tended during his career.

Within the first couple of years of Captain Bill's service, one of the area's most noted shipwrecks was registered in the waters of Lake Michigan. The *L.C. Woodruff* was a wooden barkentine built in 1866 and registered at 548 tons gross weight. On October 31, 1878, while on a trip from Chicago to its home port of Buffalo, New York, the vessel, loaded with corn, ran into trouble near Milwaukee and drifted across the lake to rest near the White River Light Station. By the next day, the ship had struck bottom in about thirteen feet of water and began to break apart.

U.S. Lighthouse Society documents state that Captain Bill observed the situation from atop the lighthouse tower and requested the dispatch of a tugboat and the lifesaving crew from Grand Haven, along with lifesaving gear and a Lyle gun. According to the National Park Service at NPS.gov, officer David A. Lyle developed the Lyle gun in the 1870s as a "small cannon that shot a projectile, to which a light line was attached, to a stranded vessel. The ship's crew pulled progressively heavier lines from shore or another ship; then a breeches buoy suspended from a rope carried one person at a time from the ship to safety."

It is said three attempts were made by the captain, his assistant keeper (and oldest son) Thomas and a group of local men to reach the ship and rescue its crew. Efforts were repeatedly thwarted by the weather. In the end, the captain of the *Woodruff* and three of the crewmen made their way to safety, while the last two men on board drowned.

Captain Bill received much praise for his decisive actions to call for assistance. Thomas was awarded a citation for his lifesaving work that day, and he would later go on to serve at the Green Island, Menominee Pierhead, Manistee and Muskegon lighthouses, retiring from service in 1928.

William Bush (son of Captain Bill's oldest daughter, Mary Ann, also known as Polly) also began his career at White River as an assistant keeper. In 1910, Bush moved into the lighthouse with his wife, Rebecca, so that she could assist with the housekeeping while also looking after the seventy-nine-year-old head keeper.

The following year, Bush was noted as the assistant keeper of record, while his often-cantankerous grandfather remained an integral part of the daily operation of his light. Bush was regarded as the keeper in title only, since Captain Bill refused to give up his role despite increasing health problems.

In late 1918, the Lighthouse Service increased its efforts to force Captain Bill into retirement, and the first entry in the official log in 1919 was signed by William Bush. The countdown was on, and Robinson was asked to leave his post and his light in early April. The night before he was to vacate, on April 2, the captain passed away in his sleep. He was eighty-seven years old and was noted as the oldest keeper on active duty in Michigan at the time of his death.

Both Bill and Sarah are buried across the channel in Montague's near-abandoned, overgrown and supposedly haunted Mouth Cemetery. Her tall, moss-covered marker is aged as one would expect after more than 120 years, and to her right side is a modest tombstone etched simply: WILLIAM ROBINSON 1831–1919.

A larger and broken headstone—with a large anchor engraved along the top portion—also bears the name W. Robinson, and some online sources credit it as being that of the former keeper. However, the date of death on

Bill and Sarah Robinson, along with his parents and at least one of their thirteen children, are buried at the Mouth Cemetery in nearby Montague. *Author's Collection.*

this Robinson is February 29, 1872, at the age of seventy-one years, eight months and twenty-seven days, before the captain even began his service at White River Light Station. This grave belongs to William Robinson II (Captain Bill's father); his mother, Ann (April 9, 1807–April 30, 1888), is also buried here, as is Bill and Sarah's eighth-born child, eighteen-year-old Annie (1866–1885). The Robinson family has been laid to rest in a somewhat fenced-in section of the cemetery directly back from the historical marker erected at the main entrance.

William Bush spent his entire lighthouse career just where his grandfather did at the White River Light Station. He retired in 1943 at the age of seventy and passed away ten years later. In all, Captain William Robinson III and his descendants served more than seven decades at this one Michigan lighthouse.

A small list of civilian keepers tended White River Light Station between 1943 and 1960, when it was decommissioned. During that time, the Sylvan Beach Association raised $6,000 to purchase the lighthouse to convert it to a museum under the management of Fruitland Township. The original Fresnel lens—which had been removed, crated and shipped to the Detroit Coast Guard Depot after decommissioning—was returned to its rightful home in 1972. However, to protect the fragile and expensive French-constructed lens, it was removed from the tower and displayed on the first floor of the museum.

In 2012, the Sable Point Lighthouse Keepers Association added White River Light Station to its portfolio (along with Little Sable Point Lighthouse in Mears and Big Sable Point Lighthouse and Ludington North Breakwater Light, both in Ludington). The White River Light Station & Museum is open daily from 10:00 a.m. until 5:00 p.m. from Memorial Day weekend through the end of September, with limited days and hours in the month of October.

WHITE RIVER LIGHT STATION & MUSEUM
6199 Murray Road
Whitehall, MI 49461

3

SOUTH MANITOU ISLAND LIGHTHOUSE

I t is common belief that the ghosts that haunt any building or location are spirits at unrest, either as the result of tragedy or a dedication to service that extends beyond human life. Such is the case for the South Manitou Island Lighthouse, where one of its most noted keepers and his wife are among the possible ghosts that reside here more than 140 years after their deaths.

The entire island is shrouded in intriguing and spirited theories that would make even the most seasoned ghost hunter's hair stand on end. Over the years, visitors have reported hearing the echo of voices, the sounds of footsteps and other unexplained noises coming from the causeway that connects the boarded-up keeper's residence to the light tower, as well as accounts reported in other nearby structures.

The *Glen Arbor Sun* published a lengthy article on July 31, 2003, entitled "Mysterious, Madness and Intrigue of the Manitou Passage" by Christina Campbell that tells many ghostly tales, including accounts specifically tied to the lighthouse and Coast Guard buildings:

> *Perhaps the spookiest buildings on the Manitou Islands are the ones most heavily inhabited today: the South Manitou lighthouse and both islands' former lifesaving stations. The South Manitou light had many incarnations between its first glow in 1839 and its 1958 closure, when the National Park Service moved its rangers onto the islands. Voices and footsteps of long-dead keepers echo up and down the lighthouse tower. In the lifesaving stations,*

phantom crews still practice their lifesaving drills, ever ready for the next steamship tragedy. Rangers and visitors have clearly heard the men's crisp shouts and dialogs. A female ranger was in the shower when she heard sounds of a sudden bustle and strange male voices yelling "Hurry up! Hurry up!" Yet she knew she was the only person in the building. Another resident of the old lifesaving building had a recliner that she closed up religiously every night. But often in the mornings, the chair would be open again.

Ironically, nearly a year to the day after publication of the article, I was invited to give a lighthouse presentation to members of the Manitou Island Memorial Society at a gathering at the town hall in Empire. The next day, it was off to the South Manitou Island to tour past the remains of farmsteads, the abandoned one-room schoolhouse, the island cemetery and other historic sites that are being restored and maintained for future generations by the nonprofit volunteer organization.

That afternoon, while society members boarded the ferry back to the mainland, a friend and I settled in on the porch of the Coast Guard station building where we would reside for the next two days and nights. Not only were we granted a unique opportunity to stay in an actual island building with power, water and internet but we were also allowed access to the tower in search of its suspected spirits.

As evening approached, one of the rangers handed over the keys to the lighthouse tower with instructions to lock it up at the end of the night, whatever time that turned out to be. After an al fresco dinner on the porch, we took the short walk to the light, unlocked the door and began our ghost hunt.

Slowly we began our climb up the 117 metal-grated spiral steps, stopping at the first landing to quiet ourselves and listen. Nothing. Making our way to the next landing, we sat and waited and again, nothing. Even at the point where the causeway connects to the keeper's dwelling, where the sounds of voices and cries had been reported by others before us, we were met with nothing but silence.

It must have taken at least an hour to actually make it to the top of the one-hundred-foot tower. To the east, freighters made their way through the Manitou Passage—barely moving against the backdrop of the Sleeping Bear Dunes off in the distance. We scooted around to the opposite side of the tower, sitting with our backs to the white-painted brick as the sun began to set in the west. And while we soaked up the visual images, we continued listening for the sounds of the spirits that were rumored to haunt the light. Still, nothing.

South Manitou Island had the only deep natural harbor within the Manitou Passage. A one-hundred-foot lighthouse tower and keeper's residence were active here from 1871 until 1958. *National Park Service.*

Even as the full moon rose in the sky that night of Saturday, July 31—a giant "blue moon" (the second full moon of the month)—and as we consumed a bottle (or perhaps two) of Michigan wine, we sadly could not lure the ghosts out from where they were hiding within the abandoned lighthouse.

In the mid-1800s, this remote island in northern Lake Michigan was home to some two hundred residents who farmed, logged and served the shipping industry that was growing throughout the Great Lakes. With a deep, crescent-shaped natural harbor on its east side, South Manitou Island was a popular stopping point for ships traveling from Chicago through the Straits of Mackinac to head north toward Lake Superior or south to Detroit. To aid the steamers, schooners and other vessels, a lighthouse was first constructed here in 1840.

According to the National Park Service, Aaron A. Sheridan came to northern Michigan from upstate New York around 1860 but was soon called into service as part of Company E, Thirteenth Illinois Infantry, during the Civil War. In late November 1863, he was seriously wounded during the Battle of Ringgold Gap in northwest Georgia. The bones of his lower left arm were shattered, leaving the entire appendage useless. While hospitalized in the Chicago area recovering from his injuries, Aaron met Julia F. Moore, who became his wife in 1865. He was twenty-nine and she was nineteen when they met on the first day of spring.

Despite his having no previous lighthouse experience, Aaron's courageous war record and reputable character earned him the position of the keeper on South Manitou Island, where he had family—including his father, James, who homesteaded an eighty-acre farm on the upper west side of Florence Lake.

Aaron and Julia moved into the keeper's dwelling on July 21, 1866, with Levi, the first of their eventual six sons. George was born at the lighthouse two years later in 1868, followed by James in 1870, Alfred in 1872, Charles in 1875 and Robert in 1877.

Five years after Aaron's appointment, the Lighthouse Service erected a new one-hundred-foot tower to house a third-order Fresnel lens, as well as an adjacent fog signal building. This would have created a greater challenge for Aaron in his daily duties, given that the cast-iron pail full of whale oil or lard would have been quite a load to haul up the tower steps with just one arm.

With more responsibility, Julia became an official assistant keeper of record effective September 30, 1872. She is noted as one of nearly three dozen women to hold such ranks in Michigan. Of course, she also maintained the household, prepared three square meals a day and raised their sons, making her a pioneer at multitasking.

Living on a remote island meant frequent trips to the mainland were in order, whether it was to tend to official business, pick up supplies, visit with family or see the doctor. In March 1878, a typical visit took a tragic turn for Aaron, Julia and their son, Robert, who were traveling in a small boat with island fisherman Christ Ancharson (also noted as Christen Anchersen Kragelund). Given the fact that the Sheridans were traveling with their infant son, one could speculate that the reason for the trip had to do with the health of the baby.

During this time of year, parts of northern Lake Michigan were likely still frozen, with icebergs floating along the watery route between the island and the mainland (either Glen Haven or Glen Arbor—both towns are referenced as destinations in various accounts). Upon their return trip, just off the ice-locked shoreline, a late afternoon squall came up, overturning the boat and throwing its passengers into the frigid waters.

The *Buffalo Commercial* newspaper in New York reported on the incident, in which Ancharson gave his account to another island resident, Richard Kitchen, who participated in the rescue and later relayed the story to Commander J.N. Miller of the U.S. Lighthouse Department in Detroit.

> *I, Christ Ancharson, Mr. and Mrs. Sheridan, and their baby, left Glen Arbor at 3 o'clock with pleasant weather and wind South-southwest. All went well with us until within one mile of the lighthouse, when the wind went down and one of the old seas capsized the boat, and Mr. and Mrs. Sheridan held on to the keel for an hour. The baby first died in the arms of Mrs. Sheridan and finally both she and Mr. Sheridan dropped off and*

DROWNED.

A Lighthouse Keeper, Wife and Child Drowned by the Capsizing of a Boat.

From the Detroit Post, March 21st.

Joseph N. Miller, United States Lighthouse Inspector, yesterday received the following letter, giving an account of a sad accident whereby the keeper of the light on South Manitou Island lost his life:

SOUTH MANITOU ISLAND, March 16, 1878.
To the United States Lighthouse Department:
Gentlemen—I, Richard Kitchen, do hereby take the authority to notify your department that the light-keeper, Mr. A. A. Sheridan, as well as Mrs. Julia Sheridan, were drowned in the lighthouse boat at 6 o'clock last evening, while coming from Glen Arbor, and within one mile of the lighthouse. The boat upset. Following is the statement of the survivor who was picked up by our boat:

"I, Christ Ancharson, Mr. and Mrs. Sheridan, and their baby, left Glen Arbor at 3 o'clock with pleasant weather and wind South-southwest. All went well with us until within one mile of the lighthouse, when the wind went down and one of the old seas capsized the boat, and Mr. and Mrs. Sheridan held on to the keel for an hour. The baby first died in the arms of Mrs. Sheridan, and finally both she and Mr. Sheridan dropped off and sank. Then I was left alone. I cried for help about four hours and-a-half, and at last my screams were heard about 10 o'clock P. M., when a boat came to my assistance. I was almost gone when they rescued me."

We will notify the friends of the unfortunates as quickly as possible.
Respectfully, RICHARD KITCHEN.

Mr. Sheridan, the light-keeper referred to, was formerly a resident of this city. He served in the army, and received wounds in the late war which unfitted him for active employment. He has been keeper of the lighthouse at Manitou since the fall of 1868. He leaves four children, none of whom is over 10 years of age.

Tragedy struck the family of Aaron and Julia Sheridan, keepers of the South Manitou Island Lighthouse, when their small boat capsized in March 1878, taking their lives and that of their infant son, Robert. *From the* Buffalo Commercial.

sank. Then I was left alone. I cried for help about four hours and-a-half, and at last my screams were heard about 10 o'clock P.M., when a boat came to my assistance. I was almost gone when they rescued me.

The *Chicago Tribune* also published an account of the accident on March 19, 1878 (reprinted on March 23, 1878, in the *South Haven Sentinel*):

A small boat left Glenn [sic] Haven at 3:30 o'clock p.m. on the 15th, containing Mr. Sheridan, lighthouse-keeper on South Manitou Island, his wife, one child and a Norwegian. When within one mile of the island the boat capsized, and Mr. and Mrs. Sheridan and the child were drowned. The Norwegian clung to the boat, and his cries for help brought a man out in a skiff, who rescued him. Mr. and Mrs. Sheridan leave a family of five small children, the oldest being only about twelve years.

According to a three-page essay published on ManitouIslandsArchives.org:

Chris Ankerson [sic], an Island fisherman with boating experience, might have been recruited for the voyage because Aaron was not a sailor. Or perhaps it was because Aaron Sheridan was partially disabled, having lost most of the use of his left arm in the Civil War, while the keeper's boat, probably a Mackinaw boat or Collinwood skiff, needed at least one fully capable sailor, and preferably two. Such boats have been described as "canoes with a sail and centerboard," and were rather notorious for easily capsizing.... Of the incident, he would later report: "They went for the purpose of taking over government mail or papers, as I understood, and were drowned by the capsizing of their boat on their return. I was with them when they drowned; I went with them on the trip to assist in handling the boat: I have always been used to boats, and I consider this boat unsafe and entirely unfit for the station. She has always been considered a dangerous boat and one that would not stand heavy seas."

At the time of the accident, the two oldest Sheridan sons—Levi, twelve, and George, ten—apparently watched helplessly from atop the lighthouse tower. It all happened so quickly that no one from the lighthouse, the lifesaving station or the small island village was able to get to the boat or its passengers in time.

Over the following weeks, islanders reported seeing the Sheridan boys walking the shoreline hoping the bodies would wash ashore. Aaron's hat and coat did show up on the beach within a few days of the accident, but the bodies were never recovered. Many years later, it was reported that a U.S. Lighthouse Establishment stopwatch, likely once part of Aaron's uniform, was found in the sand on the island by a man named Ronald Rosie.

Julia's half sister made the trip north to the island to pick up the five orphan boys (aged three through twelve) and delivered them to Bristol Village, Illinois, to be raised by their maternal grandparents, Henry and Julie Moore. An essay on the Sheridan family published on ManitouIslandsArchives.org reveals that in June 1880 "the U.S. House of Representatives of the 46th Congress received a recommendation on the bill HR2945 from the Committee on Invalid Pensions to grant a gratuity pension to support the boys until they came of age, based upon findings that Aaron and Julia were traveling on U.S.L.H.S business at the time of their deaths, and in a government vessel known to be much less than seaworthy."

Aaron's first cousin Lyman Sheridan became the next head keeper of the lighthouse, moving there from the mainland community of Port Oneida with his wife, Mary, and their four children. The family lived and worked the light for four years before Mary contracted pulmonary tuberculosis (also known as consumption), which Lyman was convinced was caused by the dampness of the keeper's residence. He resigned his position on June 2, 1882, and the family moved back to the mainland, where Mary died just a few months later, leaving Lyman to care for the children, aged five to seventeen.

Two of Aaron and Julia's sons followed in their footsteps in the lighthouse service. Alfred (known as Alf) initially served under his uncle, Edwin Moore, at the Grosse Point Light Station in Evanston, Illinois. His career was short, and he resigned after just one year.

George Sheridan had an eighteen-year career serving at the Chicago Harbor Light, Calumet Harbor Light and Michigan City Lighthouse. He was also the only officially trained keeper at the Kalamazoo River Light Station in Saugatuck (no longer standing), which he operated from 1909 until 1914. He lived there with his wife, Sarah, and their three children.

Prior to the decommissioning of the Saugatuck light in the fall of 1914, George suffered a nervous breakdown and was hospitalized for depression at the Lake Shore Sanitarium near Chicago. During those final months, Sarah became a temporary keeper, helping finalize details and close up the light. Meanwhile, George was scheduled to become the keeper of the pier lights in St. Joseph as soon as he was feeling up to it. Unfortunately, that never happened.

A newspaper article in the *Detroit Free Press* on March 1, 1915, reported that the government stopped George's salary payment on January 1 of that year due to his inability to take over his new appointment. Apparently other lighthouse keepers in the area felt for him and took up collections on his behalf to help him get by.

Just a few weeks later, on Tuesday, March 23, George went to visit his uncle Edwin at the Grosse Point Lighthouse (the same light where George's brother Alf briefly served). Years of depression over the death of his parents and younger brother, along with the fact that his wife and children opted to not join him in his transfer out of Saugatuck, became more than he could handle. That day, George was last seen going for a walk and was later found hanging from the rafters in one of the outbuildings on the lighthouse grounds.

Following George's death, Lewis M. Stoddard, inspector for the Twelfth District, wrote, "Mr. Sheridan was considered one of the best and most trustworthy employees in the lighthouse service and this office deeply regrets his loss."

Casual rumors of a ghost haunting this lighthouse have appeared on a handful of websites, although Donald Terras, director of the Lighthouse Park District at the Grosse Pointe Lighthouse National Landmark (which is located, ironically, on Sheridan Road), has disputed such stories: "I have lived here for 35-years and I can with authority say there is no paranormal activity in the buildings on Grosse Point. My standard line when people inquire is that the only person haunting this place is me."

Like many of the beacons around the Great Lakes, the South Manitou Island Lighthouse was deactivated in 1958, and over the years of abandonment, it fell into disrepair. With the establishment of the Sleeping Bear Dunes National Lakeshore on October 21, 1970, the lighthouse had a new owner, and it is now part of one of Michigan's most active summer tourist destinations.

About that same time, a group of former islanders began to gather with thoughts of protecting the historical and natural integrity of their former home. By 1988, the South Manitou Memorial Society (now known as Manitou Islands Memorial Society, representing both islands) was formally organized and began working with the National Park Service on preservation and restoration efforts.

Renovations to the lighthouse tower, causeway and keeper's residence have progressed slowly over the decades, given that permissions must first be granted by the National Park Service coupled with the fact that there is often a lack of monies available for such projects.

After a successful fundraising campaign organized by the Manitou Island Memorial Society and the Manitou Island Transit, the lantern room and spiral staircase were restored in 2008. A highlight of the project was the installation of a replica of the third-order Fresnel lens created by Artworks Florida.

On Saturday, May 30, 2009, the National Park Service hosted a ceremony in which it once again illuminated the South Manitou Island Lighthouse. Jack Sheridan, an active member of the Saugatuck-Douglas Historical Society and great-grandson of keeper Aaron Sheridan, made history when he flipped the switch of the new solar-powered light.

"As you would guess, South Manitou Island is a special place for the Sheridan family, being history buffs and all," Jack said a few years earlier in a 2006 email.

In 2006, the family finally received permission to place memorial gravestones in the South Manitou Island Cemetery to honor Aaron, Julia and Robert Sheridan. Their bodies were never recovered, and as such, no funeral or burial service was ever held. It would be 128 years before the former keeper, his wife and young son would formally be memorialized on the island they loved.

The Sheridan family spent several years trying to get the markers erected on the island, but its location inside a national park halted their efforts. The islands became part of the Sleeping Bear Dunes National Lakeshore in the 1970s, and federal regulations prohibited the placement of memorial stones within national park lands, although exemptions could be granted under proper circumstances.

During the summer of 2005, Jack's nephew Aaron (named after his great-great-grandfather and son of Jack's brother, former Allegan County district

In 2006, these memorial grave markers for Aaron, Julia and Robert Sheridan were placed in the South Manitou Island Cemetery by their descendants, *from left to right*, Chuck Zolper, Brendt Sheridan, Jack Sheridan, Sean Marin, James Sheridan and Stephen Sheridan. *Jack Sheridan.*

court judge Stephen Sheridan) discovered that the Veterans Administration would allow a memorial gravestone for the elder Aaron because he was a veteran of the Civil War. The family purchased a second memorial stone in honor of Julia and Robert to be placed next to Aaron's.

"The memorial gravestone is a long overdue tribute to Aaron Sheridan for his service and untimely death," according to an April 12, 2006 news release from then U.S. representative Peter Hoekstra, who represented Michigan's Second Congressional District from 1993 until 2011 and who helped petition the National Park Service on behalf of the family. "It will help to preserve the legacy of a dedicated keeper of a lighthouse that in its day was one of the most important on the Great Lakes."

Those interested in a unique experience (and perhaps even a ghostly encounter) should look into serving as a volunteer keeper at South Manitou

Island's historic lighthouse—one of only a few locations in the state where such an offer is available.

In 2016, Jonathan S. Schechter (a noted emergency room paramedic with twenty-five years of medical experience) shared a short blog post on the Oakland County, Michigan government website OaklandCountyBlog. com under the headline "Reflections on Simplicity and Voices of the World of Nature." There, he chronicled his five-week summer stay on the island as a volunteer keeper when he admitted he climbed the entire spiral tower staircase 189 times (117 steps up and then down, for a total of 44,226). Certainly, someone who has spent so much time inside a supposedly haunted lighthouse must have had an encounter or two to share. A quick email to Schechter yielded a detailed response sadly void of any tall tales:

> As a bit of background, I finished my third tour of duty as the SMI lighthouse keeper almost a month ago and although I was mostly in the 1871 lighthouse tower, or snooping about the attached 1855 keepers quarters during the daylight hours (ghosts do not like daylight) to accommodate island visitors, I had on many occasions climbed the old iron steel staircase during the night to enjoy the solitude and "other worldly view" night view from the catwalk. No ghosts; but some awesome views.

He notes the tragic death of Aaron, Julia and Robert Sheridan in 1878 "certainly set the stage for ghostly encounters and heck of a good story":

> I have heard many strange and at times magical sounds from inside the tower and up on the catwalk, all caused by known or natural phenomenon; the wind rusting [sic] through trees, waves smashing against the failing breakwall, barred owls hooting about love, life and territory, coyotes yipping in the moonlight, the lighthouse door rattling in strong gusts, the muffled music of fog horns, the distant rumble of freighters, the predawn cry of loons, storm clouds at night—etc.
>
> Alas, no ghosts. Not one. Not ever. Nor have there been any ghost sightings at the island cemetery where the Sheridan family placed grave stones in 2016. I am comfortable in saying that the only folks that hear or see ghosts at the SMI lighthouse (or at any other lighthouse) are impressionable folks subject to illusions of reality, delusions, fantasy, or wishful thinking in wanting to have (create) a good story (fable) to share. I would like to certify the South Manitou Island lighthouse as 100% ghost free.

Each year, as many as nine thousand people take the ninety-minute ride aboard Manitou Island Transit from Leland to South Manitou Island for daytrips or multiday rustic camping adventures (overnight excursions on North Manitou Island are also available). While there, most take the opportunity to climb the historic lighthouse tower for unparalleled 360-degree views of northern Lake Michigan, North Manitou Island and the majestic Sleeping Bear Dunes.

Named for the Ojibwe legend of a mother bear and her two cubs that swam eastward across the great lake to escape raging forest fires, the dunes stretch for thirty-five miles through Benzie and Leelanau Counties. The towering 450-foot-tall dunes represent the mother bear that climbed to the top of the sand to wait for her lost cubs, which are depicted by North and South Manitou Islands.

This spectacular natural area was voted "The Most Beautiful Place in America" in 2011 by viewers of the ABC show *Good Morning America*. In 2014, 32,500 acres of the park were formally designated as the Sleeping Bear Dunes Wilderness by the Sleeping Bear Dunes National Lakeshore Conservation and Recreation Act.

4

WAUGOSHANCE SHOAL LIGHTHOUSE, MACKINAW CITY

In 1910, Michigan's iconic White Shoal Light—noted for its unique red-and-white candy cane stripe pattern—was completed to guide ships safely through the often-treacherous waters of the Straits of Mackinac. Shortly after that, the nearby Waugoshance Shoal Light, located off the coast of what is now Wilderness State Park, became an excess navigational aid and was decommissioned by the U.S. Lighthouse Service (also known as the Bureau of Lighthouses).

However, that's not quite the story you'll get when you ask locals why the light was extinguished. Legend has it that Waugoshance, commonly referred to as "Wobble Shanks" and meaning "Fox" according to Native Americans, was so haunted that they had trouble getting and keeping staff to tend the offshore light.

Shrouded in mystery, the sixty-three-foot Waugoshance Shoal Light was constructed in 1850 to replace the wooden lightship *Lois McLain*, which had guarded this rocky shoreline since 1832. Captain Augustus Canfield of the Corps of Topographical Engineers was placed in charge of constructing the light for an elevated cost of $83,945. The foreboding tower, with its unique birdcage-style lantern room and a fourth-order Fresnel lens, was lit in 1851, becoming the first light built on the Great Lakes to be totally surrounded by water.

Rumor has it that one of the work crew died during the construction of the light, his cries still heard lofting through the now abandoned tower. Although no record of such an accident can be found in any Michigan newspapers nor in any federal documents that chronicled the lighthouse activities and histories, the lowly sounds of this lost soul remain.

In a booklet published in the early 2000s titled *James Davenport—First Keeper of Little Sable Point Lighthouse 1873–1879*, May A. Dietrich (wife of David A. Dietrich, great-great-nephew of the keeper) included a brief family account from Waugoshance, where James began his forty-eight-year Michigan lighthouse keeper career. During the summer of 1883, his younger brother, Andrew Jackson Davenport, served as second assistant keeper. It was during that two-month stretch that Andrew's wife, Clara (Hamann) Davenport, reported unusual activity, according to Dietrich's publication.

> [Clara] *found the lighthouse to be a very lonely place and she even believed it to have been haunted. She claimed doors opened without human assistance and it was full of creaks and groans. She was afraid to stay alone and when her husband went to perform his duties in the tower, she would climb the stairs with him, holding his hand all the way!*

At that time, Thomas Marshall was the head keeper at Waugoshance. He first arrived as an acting keeper on October 18, 1882, and was promoted the following June. Marshall's life ended tragically when he drowned while returning to the lighthouse on May 28, 1886. According to an article published in the *Chicago Tribune* on the day of his death:

> *Thomas Marshall of Mackinac Island, keeper of Waugoshance light, left Mackinac Island for his light this morning with a sail-boat in tow of the Propeller* E. Faxton. *On account of the heavy sea the propeller parted the line and Marshall was seen to raise sail. This was the last seen of the boat until the ferry* Crysler *picked it up about a mile off Mackinac Island. Marshall is supposed to have been drowned.*

Another brief was published the next day stating that his boat was found empty and that he was believed to have fallen overboard, leaving "a family at Mackinac Island in poor circumstances." Although his body wasn't recovered, the forty-eight-year-old Marshall has a grave marker in the Protestant cemetery on Mackinac Island. Perhaps his soul is among those that call Waugoshance home to this day.

There is more than one version of what happened to the lighthouse's most infamous keeper, John Herman, who first arrived at Waugoshance in April 1887 as an acting second assistant keeper (coming from Big Sable Point

Michigan—A Light-House Keeper Drowned.

ST. IGNACE, Mich., May 28.—[Special.]— Thomas Marshall of Mackinac Island, keeper of Waugoshance light, left Mackinac Island for his light this morning with a sail-boat in tow of the Propeller E. Faxton. On account of the heavy sea the propeller parted the line and Marshall was seen to raise sail. This was the last seen of the boat until the ferry Crysler picked it up about a mile off Mackinac Island. Marshall is supposed to have been drowned.

In 1886, Thomas Marshall became the first keeper to die during service at Waugoshance Shoal Lighthouse just outside of Mackinaw City when his boat capsized and he was lost at sea.
From the Chicago Tribune.

Lighthouse in Ludington, where he had served as an acting first assistant since September 9, 1886).

Herman steadily moved up the ranks at Waugoshance, being named head keeper in 1892. During the thirteen years he served, he was assisted by four men: Michael McIntyre, Joseph Wilmat, Louis Beloungea and Joseph W. Townshend (who would go on to tend, die at and later haunt the Seul Choix Point Lighthouse in Gulliver, also featured in this book).

When on leave, Herman often spent time on nearby Mackinac Island, where his twin sister, Mary Gallagher, ran a large boardinghouse with her husband, Thomas, and their children. Fortunately, Herman wasn't an overnight guest in August 1900, when a fire completely destroyed the home and another one next door. Tragedy would, however, strike the family twice within sixty days.

It appeared to be common knowledge of the day that Herman had two pastimes outside of tending his light. One was a good practical joke, and the other was a good stiff drink. On one fateful night in the fall of 1900, those two things didn't mix well for the forty-one-year-old keeper.

On Sunday, October 14, it has been noted that Herman was likely returning from his latest bender in downtown Mackinaw City some fifteen miles east, traveling by foot, horseback or wagon. Upon arrival back at the light, he was compelled to lock one of his assistant keepers in the tower (either Beloungea or Townshend, based on service dates compiled by Phyllis L. Tag of Great Lakes Lighthouse Research and published on TerryPepper.com).

The men who served with him over the years were accustomed to his shenanigans, but on this particular night, his antics didn't go over very well. The assistant made his way to the top of the tower and began yelling down below to Herman, who was last seen staggering around the cement crib laughing hysterically at his own clever prank.

"John Herman you let me out of here," were the suspected cries that echoed out over the waters of Lake Michigan. "John Herman, this isn't funny...let me out, now!"

Several hours are believed to have passed before the assistant sent some type of distress call to one of the nearby lighthouses. Although no accounts have been found to indicate who actually came to his rescue, one might deduce that it was Captain James Davenport, who served at the nearby McGulpin Point Lighthouse more than a dozen miles away by land (the same Davenport who had tended at Waugoshance from 1871 to 1873).

Once freed from his locked perch, the furious assistant and his rescuer set out in search of Herman, but he was never to be found, alive or dead. The only logical explanation was that during his drunken stupor, he had carelessly fallen over the edge of the crib and drowned.

Ironically, the man who loved spirits of the liquid kind became a spirit of the ghostly kind following his untimely death. During the last dozen years of Waugoshance's operation, countless stories came to light.

Keepers were advised against falling asleep while on duty, as chairs were known to be kicked out from underneath them or the heavy steel doors of the tower would slam loudly as if to startle someone awake. In the kitchen, silverware would rattle in the drawers, and cupboards would come open on their own. There's even a story of coal being scooped into the furnace when no one was actually holding onto the shovel.

Over time, the stories grew—both in the number and in the haunting details. Before long, servicemen would refuse to be assigned to this remote northern lighthouse for fear of what might happen to them during their stay.

What's interesting to note is that according to a brief published in both the Port Huron *Daily Herald* and *Jackson Citizen Patriot* newspapers on October 15, 1900, John Herman actually died on Mackinac Island that year of natural causes.

> *Mackinac Island, Mich., Oct. 15.—John Herman for 13 years keeper of Waugoshance lighthouse, died yesterday afternoon of heart failure. He was born here 41 years ago, and was unmarried. He made his home, when off duty, with his sole relative, a twin sister, Mrs. Thomas Gallagher, the later lost her home and possessions in the destructive fire of August last.*

A certificate and record of death issued by the Michigan Department of State's Division of Vital Statistics also supports the fact that Herman, son

It was originally thought that Keeper John Herman died by falling over the edge of the lighthouse and drowning, but he actually had a heart attack and passed away on Mackinac Island in October 1900. *Archives of Michigan.*

of Thomas and Mary (Garrity) Herman, died on October 14, 1900, on Mackinac Island.

The document also states that Herman was attended to by James H. Bogan, MD, from October 11 through October 14 before passing away at 1:30 p.m. that day. The immediate cause of death was listed as heart failure, with the disease-causing death noted as gastritis. The certificate did not mention where specifically Herman was when he died, since his sister's boardinghouse was still in ruins and he didn't own property himself on the island.

Additional information about Herman's death is documented by the St. Anne Catholic Church on Mackinac Island. However, in the "Record of Interments," he is listed as dying one year later, on October 14, 1901, and being buried on October 16.

That log notes that priest Francis Xavier Becker, who served at the church in 1900 and 1901, gave Herman his last rites. Unfortunately, the book of tombstone recordings published in 1982 does not list the keeper's name. It is assumed that he was buried in St. Anne's Cemetery, one of three cemeteries on Mackinac Island; however, no grave can be found.

Mary Herman Gallagher is listed in the records for St. Anne's Catholic Cemetery in the Gallagher plot, located in the east corner of the cemetery near the Tribal Burial Mound. In an email received in June 2018, Mackinac Island city clerk Danielle M. Wightman noted that "since he [Herman] is not listed in my headstone records, his may not exist anymore and he may be one of many unmarked graves."

In 1912, after sixty years of service and a dozen years after John Herman passed away, Waugoshance became a surplus site. On June 30 of that year, keeper Everitt Sterritt and his second assistant, Frederick Koehler, extinguished the light permanently. There it sat, a stone's throw off the coastline in Lake Michigan, lost and alone.

While a headstone for John Herman cannot be found, interment records indicate he was buried in St. Anne's Catholic Cemetery on Mackinac Island. *Author's Collection.*

Over time, the abandoned light was subjected to the elements—the harsh winters of the Straits of Mackinac as well as senseless acts at the hands of vandals. Broken windows, doors and holes in the roof meant that rain and snow, as well as birds, bugs and other critters, could gain access to the once-majestic light to do their own damage.

During World War II, Waugoshance found a new purpose, although it wasn't as romantic or protective as its original service had been.

According to historian Terry Pepper, executive director of the Great Lakes Lighthouse Keepers Association, the remoteness of Waugoshance in the northern Great Lakes made it attractive to the U.S. Navy, which had converted a couple of old side-wheel steamers into aircraft carriers called *Wolverine* and *Sable* to train pilots in takeoffs and landings.

As the Japanese began to use kamikaze pilots as weapons, the United States had to think of ways to combat such actions. Using advances in technology brought to it by RCA radio, the navy provided the funding to launch a remote-control drone bombing program in 1942 that was tested in northern Lake Michigan—using the ruins of Waugoshance Shoal Light as the target.

"With the breakout of World War II, hotshot flyboys decided that the old [Waugoshance] lighthouse would make a perfect target for bombing practice during their military pilot training," Pepper wrote on his website, TerryPepper.com.

Over the course of three months, countless bombs, torpedoes and drone planes waged war on what remained of the light before the program was deemed a success.

"Apparently, a number of missiles hit their target, as a massive fire broke out on the structure, completely gutting the interior of the tower and keeper's dwelling of anything combustible," he wrote.

At that time, testing operations moved to the islands in the Pacific. However, the drones were only used a couple of times before the United States dropped the atomic bomb on Hiroshima, effectively ending the war.

Back in Michigan, Waugoshance was once again at the mercy of whatever Mother Nature and civilization threw at it. It continued to fall apart, piece by piece, deteriorating beyond repair.

"In early 1983, the bullet-riddled boilerplate shell began to peel from the structure, once again exposing the soft brick to the elements," Pepper noted. "Over the intervening years, the entire casing has fallen into the lake. Anything of value remaining after the strafing exercises has been either removed or destroyed by vandals."

For obvious reasons, *Lighthouse Digest* has placed Waugoshance on its "Doomsday List"—one of six endangered lights in Michigan ranked for their deteriorated condition (the others being Charity Island Light, Fourteen Mile Point Light, Gull Rock Light, Manitou Island Light and Poverty Island Light).

In 1998, local resident Chris West organized the Waugoshance Lighthouse Preservation Society as a 501(c)(3) nonprofit organization with a lofty goal of not only preserving the all-but-forgotten beacon but also restoring it for future generations.

Shortly after that time, the U.S. Coast Guard, which had taken ownership of all the lighthouses in the country during the 1930s, finally decided to

During World War II, the deactivated and abandoned Waugoshance Shoal Lighthouse was used for bombing practice. Today, it stands in ruins off the coast of Wilderness State Park. *Marge Beaver.*

wash its hands of the dilapidated structure as part of the National Historic Lighthouse Preservation Act: "The property is offered 'AS IS' and 'WHERE IS' without representation, warranty, or guarantee as to quality, quantity, title, character, condition, size or kind."

Since acquiring ownership of Waugoshance, West (who also owns and operates Ugly Ann Boat Cruises out of the Straits of Mackinac) has worked tirelessly to clean up the site, removing countless loads of debris from both the water and the crumbling concrete crib. During that time, he admits that he has had a handful of encounters with the resident ghost—whether that is John Herman or some other unsettled spirit.

One such story was originally published in 2009 in the *Graphic*, a weekly entertainment newspaper out of Petoskey:

> *In 2001 West went out to Waugoshance alone to do some work on the property. The midday breeze had shifted without him realizing, and when he noticed, he went to check on the boat, which at this point should have been pushed into the rocks. As he approached the boat, he noticed it wasn't tied where he'd left it. And as he got closer, he saw the boat was tied up with a knot he'd never seen before. "I untied it and got out as fast as I possibly could," West recalled. Since that day, West says he leaves a bottle of Jack Daniels at the lighthouse on the last trip out for the season, as a sort of peace offering. And every year, upon return to the lighthouse, the bottle is in the same spot, cap on, but never full. "It's worked for us so far so we're going to keep going with it," West said.*

During the summer of 2013, Georg Schluender, a northern Michigan freelance writer and operator of Michigan Silent Sports, shared his experiences at Waugoshance on MackinacJournal.com:

> *The Ghost of Waugoshance hasn't decided if he loves me or hates me. Though the lives that have been lost or scared off by mysterious occurrences surrounding the lighthouse makes me believe it is he that keeps me afloat. Paddling these waters twice a year for over a decade, I've learned of the best equipped kayakers dying and qualified outfitters being rescued by the Coast Guard.*
>
> *Once not knowing how I washed to shore, I regained consciousness throwing up water. During a spring thaw, ice began to confluence around the kayak a few hundred yards from Waugoshance. Dragging myself to shore over ice haphazardly in retreat, I started to believe Woobleshanks doesn't want me in the lighthouse.*
>
> *My last attempt on Thanksgiving Day started calm, and as I put my hand on the ladder, a rogue wave slammed me and my kayak into the lighthouse crib. Still tethered to my kayak I floundered like a fish as someone laughed out loud.*

Given Herman's propensity for practical jokes, one could surmise that it is he who still taunts Schluender during his annual pilgrimages to the ruins of Waugoshance.

Waugoshance Lighthouse isn't open to the public but is visible from the shoreline near Wilderness State Park. Those wishing for a water view can take one of the Western Straits Cruises aboard Shepler's Ferry Service out of Mackinaw City (which also passes by St. Helena Island Lighthouse, Grays Reef and White Shoal). Other cruises are also offered to remote lighthouses throughout the summer season.

5

SEUL CHOIX POINT LIGHTHOUSE, GULLIVER

C hris Struble, president of the Michigan Hemingway Society, is known to savor a good cigar now and again. He also leads haunted tours with his company, Petoskey Yesterday. It makes sense then that he would be drawn to the ghost of John Joseph Willie (sometimes spelled Willy or Willey) Townshend (also spelled Townsend), the former keeper at Seul Choix Point Lighthouse.

One hundred years after his death, Captain Townshend still enjoys a stogie inside his historic lighthouse, even though his wife, Ruth, never allowed such activity while they were alive. One could almost imagine this smug ghost of a man drifting through the lighthouse puffing on his cigar without a care in the world, because in the afterlife, his wife has no control over his smoking habits.

Struble says he experienced this aromatic spirit during multiple visits to the remote light that sits at the top of Lake Michigan in Gulliver, Schoolcraft County, in Michigan's Upper Peninsula:

> *My daughter and I have spent years touring lighthouses and are quite aware that many seemed to have a common reputation for being haunted. Seul Choix seemed to be a lighthouse we visited over and over because of its unique history and location. I had spent quite a bit of time in the main house and generally always felt at ease, despite the tales I had heard from the caretakers and grounds people that usually involved cigars and cigar smoke attributed to lightkeeper Willie T.*

Tour guide, ghost hunter and historian Chris Struble of Petoskey has had only one encounter with the cigar-smoking ghost of Captain Joseph Willie Townshend at Seul Choix Point Lighthouse in Gulliver, but one was enough. *Chris Struble.*

> *One day, after having spent much of the afternoon exploring the lighthouse and surrounding area, I just had to have a few more minutes inside to myself before departing. As I was preparing to leave the farthest bedroom on the upper floor, I was overwhelmed not by the odor of old smoke from days gone by reported by so many others, but also the distinct smell of a fresh cigar passing right under my nose. That continued to dominate my sense of smell as I rushed out of the room toward the stairs, which now seemed so much further away in my heightened state of accelerating panic than when I had ascended them minutes before. I had finally had my own encounter with the former keeper!*

And Struble isn't alone.

Tim Ellis, founder of the Upper Peninsula Paranormal Research Society, says that one time while he and his ghost-hunting pals were outside smoking cigars in a tribute to Townshend, they noticed one of the curtains pulled back as if someone were watching from inside the lighthouse. But no one else was there, and they had the distinct feeling that it was the keeper spying on them.

According to an article by Michael Purvis published on August 9, 2012, on SaultStar.com:

> *The light house is believed to be haunted by as many as four ghosts, but the most famous is Joseph Willie Townshend, who died in 1910 in the upstairs bedroom of the light house quarters.*
>
> *Legend has it Townshend liked to smoke cheap cigars, but his wife would never let him smoke in the house, only outside, on the porch.*
>
> *Ellis and his pals decided to pay tribute to the gruff light keeper one night and smoke cigars outside the building.*
>
> *"This curtain pulls back, like someone's back up there in the house pulling the curtain back to look out to see who's outside," said Ellis* [one of five people to witness the occurrence]. *"Of course, we can't see anyone looking out at us, but everyone sees the curtain pull back and it holds there and it just kind of goes back where it was."*

There is no shortage of ghost stories from Seul Choix (pronounced Sis-shwa), French for "only choice." It is said that a group of sailors of French descent named the area as it provided suitable refuge for them during a storm. When the seventy-eight-foot-tall lighthouse was built in 1895 (replacing a temporary light that was erected in 1892), it was given the French-inspired name.

From faces in the mirrors to self-rocking chairs to utensils moving in the kitchen and the undeniable smell of cigar smoke, the Gulliver Historical Society has logged hundreds, likely thousands, of ghost stories (enough to fill countless three-ring binders housed at the museum) since it took over management of the property in the late 1980s.

Often regarded as one of Michigan's most haunted lighthouses, it is believed that as many as five ghosts haunt this site. Yet with all the stories, recollections, paranormal readings and unexplained photographs, one thing remains constant—Townshend is the most active of the spirits here at Seul Choix.

In the late 1990s, one specific story was shared in detail by Marilyn Fischer, president of the society and author of the 2013 book *Spirits at Seul Choix Pointe: True Lighthouse Stories.*

One night, after the museum had closed and the volunteer staff had left for the day, strange occurrences were reported. Given its remote location and the historical value of the items within the lighthouse, a security system is in place to protect the lighthouse, its artifacts and grounds. When that safety is compromised, warning alerts are sent to the local police and Marilyn herself.

Well after midnight, the lighthouse alarm sounded, indicating that something wasn't right. When Marilyn arrived, she parked near the squad car and approached the light, where both a male and female officer were investigating the scene, checking the doors and windows to look for an entry point.

Apparently, the male officer heard noises inside the lighthouse—specifically the sound of a chair scootching back across the kitchen floor—which he attributed to the resident keeper. He relayed his theory to Marilyn when she arrived. Knowing there wasn't an actual keeper on the clock at the light at the time, Marilyn quickly deduced the culprit was Captain Townshend. She told the male officer that there wasn't anyone inside the light, hinting that perhaps what he had heard was in fact the ghost of the keeper. The officer scoffed at her insinuation as they entered the kitchen only to find one of the chairs—Captain Townshend's chair—moved back away from the table as if someone had pushed it back to stand up.

Used to the antics of the former keeper, Marilyn wasn't concerned, and the three made their way through both floors of the house and the tower of the lighthouse. Looking and finding nothing, they reset the alarm and left.

A few weeks later, history repeated itself when the alarm once again sounded, sending the same two officers and Marilyn back to the lighthouse in the wee hours after midnight. This time, as she walked past the police car, Marilyn noticed the male officer was sitting inside behind locked doors while his partner was investigating near the light. Apparently, he'd had enough of Captain Townshend during the first visit.

The two women entered the light and, after a thorough walkthrough, once again determined that no one else was inside and there was no sign of damage. They locked the door, reset the alarm and left, with Marilyn following the squad car back toward U.S. 2. A short distance down the dark dirt road, they were met by a car headed toward the light—which seemed odd at that early-morning hour. The police turned on their flashers and spotlight, determined to find out who was driving out to the remote grounds during the pitch black of night.

What they found were several teenagers, well inebriated and surely full of trouble. They were taken into custody, and weeks—maybe months—later, it was determined that these boys were responsible for a break-in at a nearby property the night of the first alarm.

If you ask Marilyn her theories about those two nights specifically, she'll tell you she believes Captain Townshend tripped the alarm in his attempt to protect his beloved lighthouse. Had Marilyn and the officers not been on

County Road 341 (Seul Choix Road) those nights, it's likely these boys could have made their way to the lighthouse, and who knows the kind of damage they could have caused. Even decades after his death, Townshend remains a diligent protector of this Upper Peninsula lighthouse.

Marilyn also shares stories about Captain Townshend and the kitchen of the lighthouse, where his ghost seems to linger, hungry for attention.

When the museum volunteers leave for the day, the individual rooms of the lighthouse are always prepared for the next day's tours. On several occasions when the volunteers return the next day, the place settings in the kitchen have been rearranged to Townshend's preference. An Englishman, he expected his table to be set with the fork placed at the top of the plate (instead of to the left, as Americans do), with the tines placed down.

Seul Choix's story, along with a handful of accounts from other haunted lighthouses around the state, has been documented by Houghton, Michigan–based filmmaker Don Hermanson of Keweenaw Video Production.

In the 2010 *Spirit Sightings and Lighthouse Ghosts*, Hermanson digs into the strange occurrences that have been reported at Eagle Harbor in the Upper Peninsula on Lake Superior; Fourteen-Mile Point, located between Houghton and Ontonagon on Lake Superior; and Rock Harbor on Isle

The kitchen at Seul Choix Point Lighthouse is one of the most active rooms for spirited activity. *Author's Collection.*

Royale National Park. The documentary features interviews augmented by reenactments to bring the stories to life.

An article by Jeremy Bonfiglio on October 7, 2010, in the *Herald Palladium* of St. Joseph, Michigan, included an interview with Hermanson about his various haunted encounters:

> *Almost all lighthouses have a ghost story. The reason the lighthouses are even there is because of all the shipwrecks in these areas. Bodies would wash up on shore and were buried in unmarked graves in the local cemetery. Maybe their spirits lingered on. Keepers were stationed at these places for a long time. They climbed the tower to light the lamp, and when daylight came they would go up to extinguish the lamp. That was their whole life. They did this daily for 10 years, 20 years. They were so attached to these places I think when they passed on they just wanted to stay there.*

In all, Hermanson has produced a five-part series about paranormal activities in Michigan; others include *True Lighthouse Hauntings Revisited, Haunted Great Lakes, Two Ghostly Lights* and *Ghost Hunting with the Upper Peninsula Paranormal Research Society (U.P.P.R.S.)*.

Why is it that Townshend seems determined to keep his presence known at Seul Choix?

The son of John and Elizabeth Mary (Willey) Townshend, the lighthouse keeper was born in Bristol, England, on November 20, 1847. He made his way to North America, marrying Mary A. Locke on April 14, 1875, in Norfolk County, Canada. Together they had three children—two daughters (Mary Elizabeth, born in 1876, and Eva Kate, born in 1881) and a son (Ivan, born in 1885, who himself became a lighthouse keeper).

Mary died on February 14, 1895, and is buried at the Cross Village Cemetery in Emmet County, Michigan (off M-119 between Harbor Springs and Mackinaw City). His second wife was Jenny Mcmamie, who passed away in 1899. Townshend's third and final marriage was to Ruth Montgomery Duvall on September 7, 1904.

Before being stationed in Gulliver, Captain Townshend served as an assistant keeper from April through August 1893 at Ile Aux Galets (Skillagalee) Light in northern Lake Michigan. His whereabouts from August 1893 until April 1899 are unknown, but on April 13 of that year, he was appointed as first assistant under the infamous keeper John Herman at the Waugoshance Shoal Lighthouse (another haunted light featured in this book) just southwest of Mackinaw City, where he served until July 29, 1901.

Captain Townshend's grave can be found at Lakeview Cemetery in Manistique, Schoolcraft County. *Author's Collection.*

Moving to Gulliver, Townshend was just the second keeper at Seul Choix, serving from July 30, 1901, until he passed away of what was presumed to be lung cancer on August 10, 1910. He is the only keeper to die at the lighthouse. Following his death, his body was taken to the basement of the light, where it was embalmed and prepared for an extensive viewing, which some say lasted as long as three months—giving his family time to make it to the remote Upper Peninsula (it would be nearly five decades before the Mackinac Bridge opened in 1957). That alone would be enough to make someone haunt the building for eternity.

Townshend's final resting place, outside of the spirited haunting that continues at the lighthouse, is at Lakeview Cemetery in Manistique in Schoolcraft County.

The Seul Choix Point Lighthouse remains an active navigational aid. Its keeper's residence and ninety-six-step tower are open for tours daily (10:00 a.m. until 6:00 p.m.) Memorial Day weekend through the end of September.

SEUL CHOIX POINT LIGHTHOUSE
3183 County Road 431
Gulliver, MI 49840

LAKE SUPERIOR

6

BIG BAY POINT LIGHTHOUSE

Only a handful of lighthouses in Michigan, such as Big Bay Point Lighthouse, run as bed-and-breakfasts. This gives visitors a unique opportunity to literally spend the night with the ghosts that are rumored to haunt this sprawling brick structure. One word of advice, however: don't read the ghost stories before going to bed at night—well, unless you plan on sleeping with one eye open all night (and yes, I am speaking from personal experience).

The lighthouse in Big Bay, about twenty-five miles northwest of Marquette in Michigan's Upper Peninsula, opened in August 1896. It operated with an active keeper until 1941, when it was automated. It has been offering overnight stays high above the waters of Lake Superior since the mid-1980s. Even on nights when there is room at the inn, there is a full house with as many as five resident spirits onsite, including one belonging to the first keeper.

H. "Harry" William Prior (sometimes referred to as William H. or William Harry and often spelled Pryor) was this light's inaugural keeper, serving just five years. He and his younger brothers, James and George, had all tended the nearby Stannard Rock Light in the middle of Lake Superior—James began his service there in 1883, followed by George in 1888 and William in 1890.

The oldest brother was known to manage his light with an iron fist, was often regarded as cantankerous and recorded in his own words that he had trouble keeping qualified assistants. He was also meticulous in the keeping of his logs, which sheds light on many of the trials and tribulations involved in tending a remote lighthouse.

On November 11, 1897, Prior noted that he left the light at 11:00 p.m. to walk to Marquette following the death of his only sister, Esther Grace Prior. He was away from the light for about a week, leaving it in what appeared to be the incapable hands of his first assistant, Ralph Heater. Upon his return on November 18, Prior entered his dissatisfaction in his log book, which was reprinted on TerryPepper.com:

> *I can not see that the assistant has done any work around the station since I left. He has not the energy to carry him down the hill and if I speak to him about it he makes no answer but goes on just as if he did not hear me, he is so much under the control of his wife he has not the hart [sic] to do anything. She has annoyed me during the season by hanging around him and hindering him from working, and she is altogether a person totally unfit to be in a place like this as she is discontented and jealous and has succeeded in making life miserable for everyone at this station.*

Prior complained about Heater on more than one occasion in his logs.

"As my assistant objects to working during the closed season, I have written to the inspector to get his opinion on the matter," Prior entered on December 27 of that year, followed by "My assistant claims now that he is unable to work as he has a lame back" on January 1, 1898.

Frustration turned to humor in mid-February when Prior noted, "Mr. Heater arrived from Marquette at 6pm and walked the entire distance of 33 miles in 12 hours, including two rest stops over an hour each…pretty good gait for a lame man" and then again on February 27, when he wrote, "Mr. Heater came across the ice to the other side of Big Bay with his wife. It is Sunday and his back is not lame today."

The keeper reported to the station on the afternoon of March 5 to find that his assistant had not finished his work but instead had gone fishing. This was still winter along Lake Superior, so that likely meant ice fishing—an interesting activity for a man who professed to have repeated back problems.

Relief, however, was in sight, as Prior reported two days later that he "received a letter from the Office informing me that my Asst. would be transferred to Granite Island, for which I have every reason to be thankful."

Stepping into the assistant role was George Beamer. But just one month in, he was called to duty during the Spanish-American War, at which time his wife, Jennie, was appointed in his place—becoming the only woman to ever serve at Big Bay (from May 12 to August 26, 1898). When George returned from service, he proved to be about as useless as his predecessor, and Prior noted that this keeper also often complained he could not work because of a bad back.

"Asst. Beamer does not take hold of his work as he should. He evidently expects me to work with him whenever he is at work, and if I do not, he leaves work and does nothing until I get back to him," Prior noted on September 19. The next month, he continued his dissatisfaction and made a record of it should documentation be necessary for the Lighthouse Service. "As Mr. Beamer always objects to my questions and resents my interference, and I have passed over his dereliction before and not caring to be constantly making reports unfavorable to him, I have written this for future reference when the inspector arrives."

Toward the end of October, Prior documented his ongoing concern about his assistant: "Asst. Beamer complains of being sick and talks of leaving the station to go home to Detroit. He is too high strung for a light keeper's asst, between himself and his wife this season I imagine that I am keeping a Home for the Helpless Poor instead of a U.S. Lighthouse. I and my family having to do the greater part of the work while they receive the pay."

Finally fed up with the lack of qualified assistants, Prior put Beamer on a steamer and sent him home on November 1, 1898. Among his final notes on this assistant, he said, "This Beamer…is without exception the most ungrateful and the meanest man I have ever met."

Ironically, one of the guest rooms at the bed-and-breakfast is named for the lackadaisical Assistant Beamer. Other rooms bear the names of Keeper McDonald, Keeper Bergan, Keeper Dufrain, Assistant Temple, Helper Fleury and Helper Brown, but no room is named after the light's most recognized keeper.

Prior then appointed his nineteen-year-old son, George Edward (also noted as Edward George), to the position, and father and son worked side-by-side for about fifteen months. In mid-April 1901, tragedy struck when George fell on the steps of the crib, cutting the flesh down to the shinbone. The keeper noted in his log on April 18 that "he will have to remain in hospital for treatment." Throughout the late spring and early summer, the younger Prior battled gangrene, which eventually ate away at the tissue of his leg and ultimately took his life. On June 13, Prior wrote, "1:30pm Keeper summoned to Marquette to bury his son who died this morning."

The certificate and record of death on file with the Michigan Department of State indicates George's cause of death at the hospital in Marquette was

George Prior, the son and assistant to Keeper H. William Prior, died from an infection after being injured on the job at the Big Bay Point Lighthouse in 1901. *Archives of Michigan.*

"tuberculosis of the hip bone" caused by the spread of infection through his leg. He was buried at Holy Cross Catholic Cemetery in Marquette, supposedly in Block 4, although his grave couldn't easily be found during a visit in the summer of 2018.

Following the death of his son, Prior slipped into a state of severe depression. He was noted as despondent, and his log entries dwindled over the subsequent months. On June 28, he was rumored to have disappeared into the woods near the lighthouse with his gun and some strychnine. Locals feared the worst, and a long search to find him, alive or dead, proved fruitless. One day that autumn, Mary and the four younger Prior children (ranging in age from two to fifteen) left on an afternoon boat to live in Marquette, where she lived until she passed away.

The following November, the *Mining Journal* reported that "the remains of Harry W. Prior, the light keeper of the lighthouse at Big Bay, who disappeared last June were found by a 'land looker' Monday in the woods. The find was a gruesome one."

The *Sault Ste. Marie Evening News* also published an article mentioning that a deer hunter (later identified as Fred Babcock) discovered a human skeleton dangling by a rope from a tree limb in the woods about half a mile south of the lighthouse. Police speculated that it was the remains of the former keeper, who had disappeared and was thought to have committed suicide eighteen months before. Apparently, there were remnants of the keeper's uniform, as well as a few tufts of his red hair, helping to further identify the body. The story ran under the headline "May Be Light Keeper Pryor's Body":

> *A man arrived in Marquette from Big Bay with a report that a skeleton had been found there, at a point about a half a mile from the light. There was a rope around the fleshless neck, it is stated, and the evidence pointed to a suicidal death of the unfortunate. It is surmised that the skeleton is the remains of Lightkeeper Pryor, who disappeared at Big Bay. It will be remembered a few months over a year ago, Mr. Pryor wandered off in a fit of temporary insanity, and was never seen again, although diligent search was made in the vicinity by the people at Big Bay, assisted by Marquette friends of the missing man. It was feared at the time that the lightkeeper had made away with himself, a suspicion that may possibly be confirmed by the investigation of the late discovery of the skeleton.*

The accidental death of George Prior followed by the suicide of William Prior aren't the only dramatic stories to come out of the small unincorporated community of Big Bay (2000 population: 285), with possible ties to the ongoing ghost stories.

The Big Bay Point Lighthouse was automated in 1941, and like so many other Great Lakes lights, it was rented out to the U.S. Army and National Guard for training purposes. During the 1950s, soldiers camped out in the meadow and woods to the west of the lighthouse while undergoing anti-aircraft artillery training. On the cliff east of the lighthouse, they installed large guns used for target shooting over Lake Superior.

It was during this time, in the summer of 1952, that thirty-eight-year-old Lieutenant Coleman Peterson, a veteran of the Korean War and an active member of the 768th Anti-Aircraft Battalion at Camp McCoy in Wisconsin, was temporarily stationed at Big Bay. While in town at the still-operating

Lumberjack Tavern, he shot and killed the owner and bartender, Maurice "Mike" Chenoweth, because he believed the barkeep had raped his wife, Charlotte Ann, earlier that evening.

Peterson was charged with murder in a well-publicized trial that today has become part of a self-guided tourist trail around the Marquette area. He was eventually found not guilty by reason of insanity after being represented by defense attorney John D. Voelker—who was later appointed by Governor G. Mennen Williams as associate justice of the Michigan Supreme Court from 1956 until 1960.

In addition to practicing law, Voelker was also an avid fisherman and author writing under the name Robert Travers. It was under this pseudonym that he penned *Anatomy of a Murder* in 1958, based on the famous Marquette County case. That in turn became an award-winning movie in 1959 starring Jimmy Stewart, George C. Scott and Eve Arden, with music by Duke Ellington.

Many of the scenes were filmed at what is now the Thunder Bay Inn, a downtown property said to be built for Henry Ford, his family, friends and colleagues. Ford had purchased Big Bay's sawmill, power plant and nearly every other building in town in 1943—part of his Upper Peninsula portfolio that amassed more than 300,000 acres. At one point, he owned more property in the UP than any other single individual.

The Big Bay Point Lighthouse was decommissioned by the U.S. Coast Guard in 1961, at which time Dr. John Pick, a plastic surgeon from Chicago, purchased the structure and thirty-three acres for $40,000. He spent the better part of seventeen years restoring the dilapidated building into his dream summer home. Poor health in his eighties forced him to sell to Dan Hitchens of Traverse City, who continued to modify the lighthouse into a corporate retreat center before the economy forced him to sell just five years later.

Norman "Buck" Gotschall and his wife, Marilyn, became the next owners of the historic lighthouse, turning it into a bed-and-breakfast. They brought back the third-order Fresnel lens from the Park Place Hotel in Traverse City and displayed it in the recently restored fog signal building. Over time, the couple acquired more property around the light, amassing close to one hundred acres that were outfitted with trails, sculptures and a landing strip to the south of the lighthouse for Buck's 1957 Tri-Pacer.

It was during the Gotschall years that the first ghost tales were reported in the media. An Associated Press wire story published on October 30, 1989, in the *Green Bay Press Gazette* (along with multiple other publications from New

York to Alabama to Oregon in honor of Halloween) said: "Gotschall insists he and his wife did not invent Pryor's ghost to drum up business. Instead, he said, the first sighting was reported shortly after the inn opened by two guests who saw the spirit walking around the lighthouse in his U.S. Life Saving service uniform."

The article also references quick and unexplained banging, running water in the basement shower and other phenomena all attributed to the former keeper.

"Every morning in the spring he wakes me up, taps me lightly and bids me to go fishing," Gotschall continued. "I know that fishing was important to a lighthouse keeper. So I have to fish every morning. I've always tried to comply. I don't want a mad ghost around."

Anne and Dennis Kirby from Plainwell spent their honeymoon in the summer of 1990 at the Big Bay Point Lighthouse while the Gotschalls were keepers. That first night, Anne remembers, they settled into their guestroom and were later awoken by the sound of something ping, ping, pinging down the stairs as if someone had dropped a marble down the steps. The next morning, she said that a single marble lay resting there on the bedside table in a small ashtray—a marble that hadn't been there the day before.

Anne and Dennis Kirby weren't alone on their 1990 honeymoon at the Big Bay Point Lighthouse Bed-and-Breakfast; one of the ghosts there made its presence known on their first night. *Anne Kirby.*

Dennis had a different kind of encounter during their stay. Inspired by the ghost stories he'd read and the somewhat spooky grounds, damp basement and creaky building, he sat down at the computer in the living room and began to peck away at a story about the spirits found within the lighthouse. Marilyn Gotschall was so impressed by what he'd written that she promptly forwarded the story to the *Porcupine Press*, an Upper Peninsula–based newspaper in Chatham. The next week, the paper published the story on the front page under the headline "Ghostly Activities at Big Bay Lighthouse":

When William Pryor arrived many years ago, little did anyone know how long he would stay as the first keeper of the light. He received a small salary and a promise to stay on as long as he was able to work.

A few years after maintaining the light with one assistant, a tragic occurrence upset his peaceful lifestyle. His son had an accident which required his being taken by boat to Marquette, dying there, being transported back, and then being buried. This caused Pryor's mind to crack. Shortly after the accident, Mr. Pryor went to an isolated area and hung himself from a tree. It's not known where he or his son are buried, but it is possible they are buried on the grounds.

Shortly after the above incidents, strange happenings began to occur. Kerosene lamps would go out, or at times would even light on their own. The big light would at times change colors, ranging from red to green to pale blue. The large boiler in the fog house would hiss and blow its horn at the first hint of rain; even without the tender being present. Once it was said that a gurgling sound would fill the sitting room nearest the shoreline. Water would seep up through the cracks in the floor. A low, groaning sound would begin and a cold chill would pass through the room. An inspection of the trapdoor in the room revealed nothing out of the ordinary. An inspection of the light found nothing amiss. An inspection of the fog house would show no one had tampered with the boiler.

One thing which did cause a panic was the time one of the children was returning from the Big Bay School. Being just before dark, the light was faint, and a being appeared to be hanging from the top railing of the tower by his hands. Running to the house, the figure on the tower disappeared. Thinking someone had fallen, the lad walked quickly around the building, but finding no body, immediately told his father. A thorough inspection revealed nothing. At times, other children would see the body hanging by its hands from a railing, always just before dark. Never did an adult witness this occurrence. It has been rumored that a man once fell to his death after cleaning the outside windows, but this is only a legend. The only certain accident recorded was William Pryor's son, but his accident was connected with the dock in some way.

After many years the lighthouse was decommissioned, the keepers left and the building was deserted. The boiler in the fog house was broken up for scrap. The great light was brought down and carted away. All became still. Occasionally, some brave souls would come up and poke around the deserted structure.

It was reported by the locals that on occasion, the light in the tower would blink on, especially during violent storms on Lake Superior. It was once reported that a ship caught in a storm was searching for a safe harbor. Thinking that the Point was such a place, it was steered away from certain destruction on the rocks by a light in the tower. However, the light was no longer being tended because there was no longer a light in the tower.

Another report tells of a couple of hunters who had been poking around the grounds and walking near the old garage. Hearing noises coming from inside, one hunter asked if anyone was there. Receiving no answer but seeing a pair of shoes under the partially opened door, the main quickly opened the door. He found no one there nor anything in the garage to make any noise.

Before the lighthouse became the current Bed and Breakfast, it was turned into a single-family dwelling. Strange occurrences began to happen again. During the restoration, power tools would stop as if the electric power was out. Lights would remain on, but saws would just stop in mid cut and drills would stop as soon as they touched the walls. Water would seep up through the sitting room floor. Upon inspection of the trapdoor, it always revealed a bone-dry cistern.

When the first guests arrived after the Bed and Breakfast opened, other strange occurrences began—the most famous being the midnight walks. Nearly every night between midnight and 1:30 a.m., the creaking from the ground floor begins. Up the stairs the footsteps come, stopping at the tower door. The sound of the door opening and closing is heard, then soft footsteps up a metal stairwell, then…nothing!

Once someone was able to converse with the "ghost" if that's what it is. A red glow was seen in the tower room, now called the library. Someone asked the ghost who it was and why it was there. The answer was "I am here until the restoration has been completed. There is something still missing which must be returned before I am able to rest."

To date, no one has been able to find the answer. The ghost did not reveal who he is, but it has been said that he occasionally wears a uniform of some *sort. What is the item or items which will allow him to rest? Is it the old log books, or the original light in the tower? Maybe the unit which controlled the blinking of the light? Could it be the structure which belonged in the fog house? Who is this visitor? Is it William Pryor? Could it be his son? Is it the person who was seen hanging from the railing? Possibly someone from ages past whose name has been lost to time?*

The housekeepers at the Bed and Breakfast occasionally have contact with him; vacuum cleaners turn on by themselves, showers turn on and off by themselves. The sound of something like marbles rolling on the floor at night awaken some of the guests.

Perhaps if you visit the Lighthouse you might be the "lucky" person picked by the resident ghost to receive his secret. Maybe he will reveal a clue to why he is here, or who he is, or where he came from.

After the article appeared, media interest in the ghostly activity at Big Bay exponentially increased. Dennis, who had written stories for summer programs as executive director of Beachwood Hills Camp in Hopkins, Michigan, was even contacted about his story with requests to reprint it here and there. It was at that time that he had to admit the entire article—every apparition and spirit sighting—was made up. A tall tale crafted during his short stay at the bed-and-breakfast lives on even now, nearly thirty years later.

In March 1992, three avid preservationists and one-time guests from Chicago—John Gale and Linda and Jeff Gamble—became the next owners of the historic light, purchasing it from the Gotschalls upon their retirement. Linda moved to Big Bay to run the business, while Jeff and John remained at their respective jobs in Chicago. Just two years later, Jeff joined his wife to become the longest-serving keepers at Big Bay.

Prior's ghost is believed to have been one of the five ghosts there during their tenure. One night, Linda was startled awake by the sound of slamming cupboards in the kitchen.

On November 24, 2007, the *Twin Cities Pioneer Press*, out of St. Paul, Minnesota, ran the story "In Search of the American Beam," in which travel writer Beth Gauper (now of MidwestWeekends.com) shared a story told to her by Linda Gamble:

"One night, I heard doors opening in the kitchen and thought it was a drunk coming back from the (nearby) Lumberjack (Tavern)," Gamble said. "I have a temper, and I stormed up, but no one was there. So I figured it must be Will, and I said, 'OK, I know ghosts don't like change, but we're

changing things. I have to get up in the morning and make breakfast, so cut it out.' Then I slammed a cupboard and went back to bed.

"The next morning, all the cupboard doors were closed, and we've never had a reputable port of Will since," she said. "I call that an Italian exorcism."

In a February 11, 1996 article in the *Star Tribune* out of Minneapolis, Minnesota, Linda also admitted she "heard him once....I think he's gone now, though. I had a conversation with him in the kitchen." As for Prior's death, Linda had her own theories. "They said it was suicide. But I wonder. He left with strychnine and a gun and ends up hung. I think he was murdered."

More than one story accounts for a tall red-headed man wearing a late 1800s uniform walking the grounds around the lighthouse, doors and windows opening and closing on their own, lights turning off and on by themselves and disembodied footsteps making their way across wooden floors.

One overnight guest reported seeing the reflection of a man wearing a keeper's hat standing behind her in the mirror. Other guests have woken

The Big Bay Point Lighthouse Bed-and-Breakfast is one of only a handful of historic inns in Michigan where guests can spend the night and imagine what life was like as an early keeper. *Big Bay Point Lighthouse.*

from deep sleep to find a man gazing at them from the end of their beds. Countless stories tie the ghosts to crew members lost at sea during nearby shipwrecks or a woman who was reportedly murdered at the light when it was abandoned in the 1950s (although no record of such a crime was found in an online search of local newspapers).

Nick Korstad stepped into the keeper role when he assumed ownership of the Big Bay Point Lighthouse on May 19, 2018. He is also the current keeper of the Spectacle Reef Lighthouse in Lake Huron. Before coming to Michigan, he bought and restored the 1875 Borden Flats Lighthouse on the Taunton River in Fall River, Massachusetts, which was featured in *Coastal Living* magazine, on NBC's *Nightly News with Lester Holt* and on HGTV's *You Live in What?*

When asked via email about any ghostly encounters, Nick said, "Unfortunately I've only been onsite since May 19 and haven't had much time to gain access to the ghostly past." But if history is any indication, it won't be long before Prior or whoever the spirits are make their presence known.

BIG BAY POINT LIGHTHOUSE
4674 County Road (KCB)
Big Bay, MI 49808

7

MARQUETTE HARBOR LIGHTHOUSE

Among the many ghosts that haunt lighthouses around the Great Lakes State are a handful of children—most often girls dressed in period clothing who find great joy in playing in and around the light and surrounding grounds. This is the case at Marquette Harbor Lighthouse along the Lake Superior shoreline.

Constructed in 1866 to replace an original 1853 structure, the current Marquette Harbor Lighthouse is regarded as one of the most vital navigational beacons on Lake Superior. A premier shipping port for iron ore on the Great Lakes, this town was originally founded as Worcester by Amos Harlow and explorer Peter White (for whom the library is named) in 1849. The following year, it was renamed after French explorer Jacques Marquette, who founded the first European settlement in Michigan at Sault Ste. Marie.

Iron ore was discovered in the UP in the mid-1850s by William Burt, and before long, the shoreline town was booming. In addition to the massive ships traveling in and out of port, roads and railroads were also put in place not only to handle the industrial traffic but also to cater to a growing number of travelers who made their way to this remote area.

Today, tourism is one of the main economic drivers, as visitors come to explore the shoreline, the famous "Blackrocks," a growing craft beer scene and the year-round outdoor recreational activities in the Upper Peninsula's largest city. Tapping into ghost tourism, Travel Marquette—the local convention and visitors' bureau—published a listing of haunted sites around

Perched on a cliff overlooking Lake Superior, the Marquette Harbor Lighthouse has guided ships since 1866. *Author's Collection.*

town on the award-winning Michigan.org that includes the Marquette Harbor Lighthouse:

> *Most look at the Marquette Harbor and its lighthouse and see the beauty of the lake, but Taylor Adams, a long-time worker at the Marquette Maritime Museum and daughter of the former Coast Guard station chief, often finds her eye drawn to a spookier apparition. On several occasions, Taylor witnessed a small ghost of a girl on the upper floor of the lighthouse. Standing in broad daylight, this ghostly figure of a girl is seen staring out the upper floor window, peering out at the horizon of Lake Superior. It has been reported that the girl prefers catching a glimpse of the horizon when Lake Superior is in a calm state, as the winds of the lake stir up the sounds of the souls of her long-lost mother and father, proving too much for her to bear.*

On Friday, June 13, 2014, ABC-10 UP visited the lighthouse looking for the young girl, who had been seen over the years by museum staff, volunteers and visitors alike. Adams again shared her thoughts on the young ghost who resides inside the lighthouse:

This little girl, her name is Jesse…she's got red hair and green eyes and she's barefoot. And she wears like a little Sunday's best dress, it looks like from about the nineteen-teens or so. She's really attracted to female figures, like motherly figures, and also children, she loves children. Lots of times you'll hear her skipping around the lighthouse and hear giggles and nobody's there. She's a really nice spirit and she's not threatening at all.

According to online research on the family trees of early keepers, a son named Jesse was born in 1856 to Nelson and Anastasia (Eliza) Truckey, who served at the original lighthouse from 1861 until 1865.

Noted as a strong Union man, Nelson took a leadership role in the Civil War, helping form Company B, Twenty-Seventh Infantry Regiment of Michigan Volunteers. The unit saw heavy action, participating in some of the most famous campaigns including Vicksburg, Wilderness, Spotsylvania, Cold Harbor and the final pursuit and capture of Robert E. Lee at the Appomattox Court House in April 1865. Nelson would become a second lieutenant and finish the war as a captain.

While Nelson was away, Eliza was named the keeper of record from November 15, 1862, until October 26, 1865, making her one of the earliest female tenders on the Great Lakes. She was also known by local Native Americans as "Mother of the Light," and rumor has it that her mediation skills resulted in several of the local men being allowed to keep their scalps after disagreements with the Natives.

While the family story is quite fascinating and the subject of a book in and of itself, it is unlikely that Jesse Truckey is the child ghost here. It's the right name but the wrong gender and time period.

Historian, author and Marquette resident Frederick Stonehouse noted during the ABC-10 segment that a daughter of one of the keepers was seriously injured here in the early 1900s—perhaps the ghost is that of this girl?

Between 1898 and 1903, Robert Carlson served as head lighthouse keeper in Marquette. He lived in the stately redbrick home with his wife, Anna Maria, and their three children: Cecilia, born on October 9, 1892, and twin boys Carl and Robert, born in 1894. A couple of black-and-white family photographs exist of the children, but obviously it's impossible to determine their hair or eye color. No known accidents happened to the keeper's daughter, and the name "Cecilia" doesn't sound anything like "Jesse," as the museum staff calls this ghost. However, the time period fits, as Cecilia was six years old when the family moved into the Marquette lighthouse and eleven when they were reassigned down the coastline to Whitefish Point in Paradise.

Cecilia Carlson and her younger twin brothers, Robert and Carl, were children when they moved into Marquette Harbor Lighthouse with their father, Keeper Robert Carlson, and mother, Anna Maria. *National Park Service.*

Many years later, on August 5, 1927, the *Oshkosh Northwestern* newspaper out of Wisconsin published a story under the headline "Member of Coast Guard Crew Save Life of Little Boy" that closely resembles the stories told about how the child in question was injured at the Marquette lighthouse—but it is about a boy who also isn't named Jesse:

> *Robert Carlson, 6, owes his life to the promptness and efficiency of E.J. Bennett, member of the coast guard crew at Marquette, Mich. Robert was playing in the rocks near the Marquette lighthouse and climbed onto a large rock some distance from shore. He slipped and fell into six feet of water. Bennett, who was on duty at the lookout tower, saw the lad slide into the water, and rushed to his rescue. He found the boy, unconscious, on the lake bottom. Bennett immediately applied first aid methods, and soon the lad recovered.*

Clearly, Keeper Carlson's namesake son would have been much too old in 1927 to be the child in question, but perhaps he had his own son named Robert? Or maybe he had a nephew born to his twin brother, Carl? Little is known about the twins (although the 1930 census indicates they were living in Chicago).

However, Cecilia's life is more documented. She married a fisherman named Ralph Endress (sometimes spelled Andress) on December 19, 1908, when she was just seventeen and he was twenty-seven. They had two children, Bertha, born in 1910, and Robert, born in 1917. Their son would have been ten at the time of the reported accident above. Is it possible the newspaper had his age wrong? The Carlsons were all living at Whitefish Point (also included in this book) in 1927, so if this child was part of the family he must have been just visiting the Marquette light the day of the accident.

Perhaps, over time, the stories have become mingled with each other. Or maybe this ghost is an entirely different child than those mentioned above.

Over the years, dozens of keepers and their families called the Marquette Harbor Lighthouse their home. According to TerryPepper.com, during

> *the transfer of responsibility for the nation's aids to navigation to the Coast Guard in 1939, a barely documented flow of Coasties operating out of the lifesaving station were assigned to assist the remaining lighthouse service keepers. With the outbreak of World War II, the station became a Coast Guard training station with up to 300 recruits living in the various station buildings. The main dwelling became the primary Coast Guard station*

housing in the 1950s and to provide easier access, an addition enclosing a stairway was added at the rear of the building.

Guardsmen and their families lived inside the Marquette Lighthouse until 1998. In 2002, the Marquette Maritime Museum signed a thirty-year lease with the Coast Guard for the lighthouse and approximately two and a half acres of picturesque Lighthouse Point. On July 30, 2016 (the 150th anniversary of the lighthouse), an act of Congress transferred the Coast Guard station property (about seven and a half acres), including the 1891 Life-Saving Service Station house, keeper's house and lighthouse, to the City of Marquette for use as a public park.

The Coast Guard still operates the light, an active aid to navigation that guides ships in and out of the harbor just as it has for 140 years. Throughout the summer season, the staff offers escorted interpretive tours through the lighthouse, its fifty-step tower and around the grounds Tuesdays through Sundays at 11:30 a.m., 1:00 p.m. and 2:30 p.m.

MARQUETTE MARITIME MUSEUM & HARBOR LIGHTHOUSE
300 North Lakeshore Boulevard
Marquette, MI 49855

8

WHITEFISH POINT LIGHTHOUSE, PARADISE

The searchers all say they'd have made Whitefish Bay if they'd put 15 more miles behind her, wrote Gordon Lightfoot in one of the most noted maritime songs in Great Lakes history, "The Wreck of the *Edmund Fitzgerald*."

On November 10, 1975, the 728-foot "Fitz" sank in Lake Superior about fifteen miles offshore from Whitefish Point Light Station, taking with it the entire crew of twenty-nine including the captain, Ernest McSorley. The *Fitzgerald* wreckage remains 535 feet below the water's surface, one of nearly 200 known shipwrecks in the area and more than 550 along an eighty-mile stretch known as "Lake Superior's Shipwreck Coast" or "The Graveyard of the Great Lakes."

According to MidwestWeekends.com, the oldest shipwreck in this area dates to 1816, when the schooner *Invincible* was lost at sea. Other noted ships to sink nearby include the *Independence* in 1853 due to a boiler explosion; the *Niagara* in 1897 as it was overloaded with iron ore and sank in a storm; the *Comet* in 1875 when it was rammed by the *Manitoba*, claiming ten lives; the wooden steamer *Osborn* in 1884, the fourth boat in a month to be struck by the steel-hulled passenger liner *Alberta*; and *Isaac M. Scott* and *John B. Cowles*, which collided in 1909 with fourteen deaths recorded and the licenses of both pilots suspended. Twenty-nine lives were also lost in 1920 when the *Willis King* and *Superior City* confused passing signals and struck each other.

It's no wonder, with so many lost lives and vessels in the vicinity, that spirits are clinging to something here at Whitefish Point. Repeated stories have

The most noted shipwreck on the Great Lakes was the *Edmund Fitzgerald*, which sank on Lake Superior off Whitefish Point on November 10, 1975. *Great Lakes Shipwreck Museum.*

surfaced about a number of ghosts and unexplained experiences within the various buildings on site. From the touch of a child to locked doors opening by themselves to voices and footsteps, Whitefish Point has a long list of encounters that would likely scare even the most seasoned captain and crew.

Established by Congress in 1849, Whitefish Point is recognized as the oldest operating light on Lake Superior and, some say, the most important, as all boats entering and leaving the largest of the Great Lakes must pass by the current seventy-six-foot tower (built in 1861) and its lighthouse complex.

The campus itself was near extinction in the early 1980s, when Whitefish Township officials approached the Great Lakes Shipwreck Historical Society for assistance in preserving the property. The U.S. Coast Guard, which had jurisdiction over the structure at the time, licensed the society to operate a museum, and the first exhibits opened in 1985.

Eleven years later, an act of Congress officially transferred the site to the society, and over the last thirty years, this organization has not only made great strides in maintaining the integrity of the lighthouse and its various buildings but has also expanded its offerings.

Guests are now invited to spend the night in the restored 1923 U.S. Coast Guard crew's quarters between late April and early November. It is here, in one of the five guest rooms, that many of the ghost stories originate.

The former Coast Guard crew's quarters at Whitefish Point now offers overnight stays for the general public, complete with ghostly experiences. *Author's Collection.*

In the summer of 2008, freelance writer and author Kim Schneider of Suttons Bay, Michigan, shared an account with Mlive.com (publishers of *Grand Rapids Press, Kalamazoo Gazette* and six other Michigan-based newspapers in Ann Arbor, Bay City, Flint, Jackson, Muskegon and Saginaw) about her weekend stay at this infamous light station:

> *Around 6 a.m., my closed, locked room door pops open. I explain it away as suction from another door, perhaps opening in the hallway. Later in the day, I meet an Illinois couple, Jody and Jerry Zamirowski, staying on another floor. I soon start suspecting a more supernatural explanation.*
>
> *Their door, they tell me over coffee, opened itself at 6 a.m. that morning, and at 6 a.m. the morning before. I mention my face stroking and find more corroboration* [referenced earlier in the article when Kim mentions a dream she has when someone is stroking her face, sweetly—like a child would do].
>
> *"I felt someone stroking my back!" Jody says.*
>
> *Most unusually, her husband tells me he glanced toward his bathroom door to see an image of a man in an old blue uniform, "like I could see it in one eye but not the other."*

Kim, curious by nature as you would expect a writer to be, began to dig into the history of the light and its past tenants when she uncovered a photograph labeled "Albert Gross, chief warrant officer" inside the crew quarters. When she asked Jerry if this was the man he had seen near his bathroom, he nodded and then pointed to his main-floor guest room door, which bore the name "Chief Officer."

When questioned about the experience some ten years later, Jerry said, "It was weird since I don't believe in ghosts. He was standing in the entrance way in a royal blue uniform. I just know that the man looked similar to a picture I saw on the wall the next day and was told he was a lighthouse captain. Doors opened and closed during the night," he continued. "Two women staying there had similar door experiences. My wife heard the doors but didn't see the man."

A photograph of Albert Gross was provided by the society and was recently shared with Jerry, who says that isn't the man he saw during his 2008 stay, indicating the ghost he saw was from the 1800s. No images of keepers from that era were readily available for comparison, and the identity of the spirit that Jerry saw remains a mystery.

Countless ghost stories from this lighthouse and many others around the state have been documented by Don Hermanson of Keweenaw Video

Production, who has produced several DVDs on the subject. One former employee said that she once sat on a bed inside the crew's quarters when she felt the gentle touch of a child's hand on her arm. She glanced over to her side and noticed a small indentation on the bed next to her left by the child's spirit.

Hermanson has also worked with the Upper Peninsula Paranormal Research Society (UPPRS)—a professional paranormal research team from Sault Ste. Marie, Michigan, and an official family member of The Atlantic Paranormal Society (TAPS) from the Syfy Channel's *Ghost Hunters*. In 2007, the two teams met up at the Whitefish Point Shipwreck Museum to document their work and subsequently created a DVD titled *Ghost Hunting with the U.P.P.R.S.* According to the DVD's online description:

> *While filming Investigation #1 in the Shipwreck Museum, Hermanson's camera recorded audio of what is believed to be a women's voice, clearly heard on the tape and by two witnesses. Several team members also had personal experiences in the museum and other buildings on the grounds. Several workers and visitors to the Shipwreck Museum complex have reported seeing ghostly images or hearing footsteps in upstairs rooms and other unexplained noises. Several weeks after documenting the group, Hermanson returned to Whitefish Point to experience heavy weather and film the complex after dark.*

One of the Great Lakes region's most noted maritime historians, author and Northern Michigan University professor Frederick Stonehouse even stated in one of the documentaries that as many as one hundred tragic deaths can be attributed to shipwrecks along this stretch of shoreline and that it is likely that many of these souls are in limbo, taking up residency in the safety of the lighthouse campus buildings.

In 2007, Stonehouse was asked to accompany UPPRS on one of its ghost hunts, and after the fact, he documented that experience in an article in *Lake Superior Magazine* (available online at LakeSuperior.com) under the headline "Do Ghosts Walk at Whitefish Point? Paranormal Experts Investigate":

> *For decades, I've researched Great Lakes maritime history and have more than a few times stumbled across tales of spirit encounters and other-worldly happenings. I've remained skeptical, but open, to reports of ghosts, phantom ships and strange occurrences.*
>
> *If there are such manifestations as ghosts, Whitefish Point is a logical place for them. It sits forlornly at the east end of Lake Superior's infamous*

"Shipwreck Coast," a 40-mile stretch littered with the hulls of long-dead ships and drowned bodies of nameless sailors.

One visiting psychic claims perhaps 50 lost spirits haunt the point, on the grounds and beach and in the buildings. Visitors and staff report a plethora of ghost sightings.

An Indian girl from times gone by has been seen inside and outside the main museum building as well as in the gift shop, office building and old fog house. Another young girl in old-time clothing has been reported wandering the grounds. A woman in 1890s dress has been spotted standing on the gallery, just outside the light tower lamp room. She stares intently out to the cold lake. Of course there are also yarns about a mysterious ghost ship, a gray schooner with all sails full and drawing, gliding silently past the beach only to disappear into nothing.

Mariners in wind-wagon days believed that wrecks with loss of life repeat in ghostly image, a continuous loop of disaster. They would see a wreck replayed and hear the desperate cries of dying comrades above the howling wind and crashing surf.

Life-Saving Service patrols at the point found bodies rolling in the wave wash after every big storm and more were chopped out of translucent winter ice. The government men dutifully carried the bodies to unrecorded graves behind the dunes to bury them in the cold sand. Do these forlorn souls wander the desolate beach, searching for shipmates or for a way home?

After several decades of researching lighthouse history, both Great Lakes and salt water, I have concluded that every one of the beacons is haunted… or at least someone believes a ghost or two is floating about. Whitefish Point is no exception.

The Motor City Ghost Hunters, out of Dearborn Heights, Michigan, have posted several detailed accounts online at MotorCityGhostHunters.com dating back to 2009. During that first visit, six of their members spent time in each building in the complex, where they experienced drastic temperature changes, rapidly fluctuating EMF (electromagnetic field) activity, odd sounds and voices, drained flashlight batteries and the feeling that someone was watching them at times.

Two incidents were noted inside the crew's quarters. One was pajamas that were moved from a pillow to the end of the bed, and the other was someone being woken up after feeling someone touch their face, arm and foot. Inside the museum, motion sensors at the back of the room were tripped for no apparent reason.

In the fall of 2010, a larger group from Motor City Ghost Hunters returned for two more days of investigation. According to the online account:

> *Teri, Cathy & Chass moved to the Museum. Both Chass and Teri reported seeing some shadow movement. After asking a few questions with no response, Chass began speaking Native American and the flashlight began blinking immediately. It seemed as though this "opened the flood gates" so to speak, to a lengthy EVP* [electronic voice phenomena] *question and answer session. After establishing a "yes & no" flash pattern, we used the flashlight as a tool, and the consistency of responses gave the impression that it was intelligent communication with a spirit. Through question & answers we determined the woman presence was that of a Native American woman who grew up in the area. We determined she lost her baby boy to an illness, which neither she nor the elders could cure. Perhaps she lingered because she was reluctant to leave her baby behind.*

In October 2013, the team posted a video to YouTube taken during one of its visits to Whitefish Point that shows a young girl dressed in a white nightgown walking through an upstairs bedroom of the light keeper's house. The story was picked up by Fox 2 News in Detroit, and the video has been shared on countless social media channels.

In an email received in August 2018 from Brenda Ozog of the Motor City Ghost Hunters, she revealed that the spirit is that of Bertha Endress, the granddaughter of Keeper Robert Carlson, captured in her bedroom at the lighthouse.

The Carlson family lighthouse stories are longstanding. Robert and his wife, Anna Maria, had served at Outer Island, Michigan Island (a detailed newspaper account of one winter spent there can be found online) and Marquette Harbor before being reassigned to Whitefish Point. Their oldest child, Cecilia, was eleven when they moved to Paradise, and her twin brothers, Robert and Carl, would have been nine.

On December 19, 1908, seventeen-year-old Cecilia married twenty-seven-year-old Ralph Endress (sometimes spelled Andress) at the lighthouse. The newlyweds lived nearby and soon began a family of their own. Bertha was just two weeks old when she and her parents moved into the lighthouse in 1910. Robert Endress was born there seven years later in 1917.

Life wasn't always peaceful in Paradise for the Endress family, and on May 4, 1920, Ralph was granted a divorce. Cecilia stayed at Whitefish Point with the children, likely relying on the help of her parents to raise them. Interestingly, the couple remarried on April 15, 1924 (Bertha would have been fourteen and Carl seven at the time). By 1930, it appears the couple has separated once again, although no formal divorce documentation is on record. According to that year's census, Ralph was living in Detroit as a millwright, while Cecilia's residency is noted at the Newberry State Hospital in Luce County.

Opened in 1895 as the Upper Peninsula Asylum for the Insane, the 11-acre complex was established on a remote 720-acre farm and housed over one thousand residents in the early twentieth century. According to her death certificate, Cecilia had been a resident of the facility for eighteen years, four months and twenty-four days, having been admitted in December 1926 and dying of pulmonary tuberculosis on March 26, 1944.

Bertha and Carl lived with their grandparents at Whitefish Point into their adulthood, which may explain why Bertha's ghost remains an active spirit at this historic light. For the first two-plus decades of her life, Whitefish Point was the only home Bertha knew. She remained dedicated to the lighthouse she was raised in, as noted in her obituary from October 2007 in the *Sault Evening News*:

> In 1980 she worked with Tom Farnquist to restore the Whitefish Point Lighthouse. Bertha provided furniture, pictures, and artwork she had retained when her grandfather retired as Lighthouse Keeper. She was very instrumental in establishing the Lighthouse quarters, offices, and museums. On the occasion of her 90th birthday, longtime friend Paul D. Freedman published a series of her short stories in a book entitled Beneath the Shining Light. The stories tell of the adventures of the sailors and her family while residing at Whitefish Point.

The Great Lakes Shipwreck Museum is open from 10:00 a.m. until 6:00 p.m. daily, May 1 through October 31. Admission includes access to the lighthouse keeper's residence, tower, museum and gift shop. The crew's quarters are only accessible to bed-and-breakfast guests.

WHITEFISH POINT LIGHT STATION
GREAT LAKES SHIPWRECK MUSEUM
18335 North Whitefish Point Road
Paradise, MI 49768

9
POINT IROQUOIS LIGHTHOUSE, BRIMLEY

Before European voyageurs discovered Michigan, Native Americans called this vast land in the center of the Great Lakes their home. The Ojibwa (Chippewa) navigated the rivers in their birchbark canoes, hunted the land and built communities, eventually becoming allies with the French explorers and fur traders who traveled to this area along Lake Superior in the early seventeenth century.

In 1662, a massacre took place along the rocky beach near where Point Iroquois Lighthouse now stands. The infamous battle was between the Ojibwa and a band of Iroquois who had invaded from western New York, some four hundred miles away. At the end of the day, the Ojibwa prevailed, and it is said that all the Iroquois braves were slaughtered on the beach, their blood seeping into the sands of time forever.

The spirits of those restless souls are believed to still haunt the grounds, which have been immortalized in the name of their defeated. The native Algonkian name for the point is Nadouenigoning, composed of the words *Nadone* (Iroquois) and *Akron* (bone), forever referring to this place as a boneyard for the Iroquois.

The discovery of copper and iron ore in the Upper Peninsula nearly two hundred years later, in 1844, necessitated a passage for ships traveling through the rapids of the St. Marys River to the steel plants of the lower Great Lakes. The St. Marys Falls Canal, commonly known as the Soo Locks, was opened in 1864 and is one of the most heavily used commercial shipping canals in the world.

The beach along Point Iroquois Lighthouse in Brimley was once strewn with the dead bodies of Native Americans after a bloody massacre in 1662. *Author's Collection.*

During this time, the U.S. Lighthouse Service appropriated $5,000 to build a small forty-five-foot wood and rubblestone lighthouse at the point, which was completed in 1856. Point Iroquois Lighthouse was outfitted with a flashing fourth-order Fresnel lens at the top of its seventy-two steps with a range of visibility of just ten nautical miles out into the waters of Lake Superior. A new light and keeper's quarters were built in 1870 to replace the crumbling original structure, this time at a cost of $18,000.

Yet despite its increased height and the reach of its light, Point Iroquois couldn't prevent all maritime accidents. In 1919, during what is often referred to as the "Gales of November," the steamer SS *Myron* (built in 1888 in Grand Haven as the wooden steamship *Mark Hopkins*) went down just north of Whitefish Point (some forty-eight miles away, by land), taking with it the lives of all seventeen crewmen. Captain Walter R. Neal was the only survivor. He was found a couple days later floating near Ile Parisienne (a remote, undeveloped Canadian island located in the middle of Whitefish Bay). One report written in 1985 by Norm Mills and featured in a historical notebook at the lighthouse museum says a few minutes prior to the sinking, the wheelsman gave the captain a chew of tobacco and that "he kept chewing on it till he was on the board of the *Franz* [the rescue ship]. They claim the chewing kept his jaws from freezing and that is what saved his life."

The crew was not so lucky. While attempts to rescue them were made, it is said they were so numb with cold that they could not catch the lines, and all froze to death in the end, still wearing their life jackets. Some men were encased in ice and found in a small lifeboat a few days later.

Another disturbing account reports that lighthouse keeper Elmer Byrnes would gather the bodies as they washed ashore, taking them to an undertaker in the nearby town of Brimley, who paid ten dollars apiece for the "floaters." However, an article published on December 4, 1919, included a sub-headline: "$25 Reward for Each Body Found After Today."

The last eight men weren't recovered until the following spring, when they had to be chopped out of the ice along the shore near Salt Point, between Whitefish Point and Point Iroquois. These men were buried at the Mission Hill Cemetery in Bay Mills Township. A memorial in the cemetery pays tribute to the men who died, with a marker that reads:

Sailors of the Steamer "Myron"

During the early evening of November 22, 1919, the steamer "Myron" slid beneath the waves of Lake Superior off Whitefish Point during a violent storm. The crew attempted to use the lifeboats while the captain chose to remain with his ship. The crew perished but the captain was found near Ile Parisienne, clinging to a portion of the floating wreckage. In the spring of 1920, eight bodies from the "Myron", encased in ice, washed ashore at Salt Point. They are buried here. May they rest in peace.

Dozens of newspaper accounts of the wreck and subsequent recovery efforts were published about the accident, many of which are included in a binder in the Point Iroquois Lighthouse Museum.

The Great Lakes Shipwreck Historical Society discovered *Myron*'s wreck in 1972 in about fifty feet of water just a couple miles from Whitefish Point. Today, it is protected as part of an underwater museum in the Whitefish Point Underwater Preserve. Artifacts gathered from the site in the 1980s are property of the State of Michigan and are on loan to the Great Lakes Shipwreck Museum, where they are displayed.

Perhaps the ghosts who haunt this section of shoreline belong to one or more of these crewmen who died one hundred years ago during this horrific shipwreck.

Atop Mission Hill, a monument pays tribute to eight men who froze to death during the November 1919 shipwreck of the SS *Myron*. *Author's Collection.*

One other young spirit is said to find solace near Point Iroquois—a young girl who, in the late 1940s, tragically lost her life just a few miles away. The presence of ghosts or unusual activity at the light hasn't been well documented over the years. However, in the 1990s, Janet Russell was volunteering there when she was visited by a clairvoyant.

"A lady came in and told me that she felt the presence of the girl near the light tower," Russell said via email. "I didn't get her name, but she came into the lighthouse late in the afternoon. She and I were the only people there. I remember her story of either seeing or sensing the little girl made the hair on the back of my neck stand straight up and it made an impression on me. Spirits are apt to go to locations that made big impression on them and for a 3-year-old, seeing the massive tower with her family would have been very impressive."

The woman's vision was, in fact, based on an actual incident that had happened some fifty years earlier. Three-year-old Carol Ann Pomranky was living with her family in a remote cabin not far from Point Iroquois when, on Wednesday, July 7, 1948, she was carried away and killed by a bear.

The *Detroit News* published an article about the accident the following day, sending the story out on its wire service, where it was picked up as far south as Florida.

Two hours after a terrified mother saw a black bear carry away 3-year-old Carol Ann Pomranky from the porch of their home, the animal was shot and killed as it returned to the body of its little victim. The tragedy, first authenticated instance in many years of a bear killing a person in Michigan, occurred 30 miles west of the Sault, within two miles of Bay Mills, a popular tourist resort on Lake Superior's Whitefish Bay. Carol's father, Arthur Pomranky, is keeper of the fire observation tower in the Marquette National Forest. The home from which she was carried is at the base of the tower. Mrs. Pomranky and a son, Allen, 5, were in the house when the mother saw the bear approach across the small clearing. Before she could go to Carol's defense, the bear had snatched the baby from the porch steps and was lumbering away on its hind legs carrying the child in its forepaws. The child probably was dead by that time, said Dr. Lyman McBride, coroner, for she was killed by a bite that sent one of the bear's fangs into her brain. Mrs. Pomranky, hysterical, telephoned the Raco Forest Ranger Station, six miles away, where her husband was working at the time. Pomranky, Bruce Elliott, ranger in charge of the station, and Wayne Weston, commercial fisherman living nearby, hastened to the home by automobile. An alarm was telephoned to the Sault, and an appeal broadcast for volunteer searchers. Alex Van Luven, veteran Forestry Service Trapper, was one of the first to arrive with his hunting dogs. While Pomranky cared for his wife, the others began the search. The dogs soon found one of Carol's shoes. Then they led the way to her body, lying a quarter of a mile in the forest, beside a stream in a small clearing. While Weston remained with the body, Van Luven moved on in search of the bear. The animal, apparently driven away from the body by the approach of the hunters, returned shortly after Van Luven left. Weston seated beside the body, opened fire with a 30-30 deer rifle, from a distance of about 30 feet. About 100 men, including State conservation officers, State Police and civilians was [sic] just beginning to scour the forest when the bear was killed. Although the animal's age was estimated at a year and a half, it weighed only 150 pounds. Hunger apparently had driven it to attack the child, the rangers said, for it was scrawny and obviously undernourished despite the abundance of berries, clover and insects, a bear's usual forage at this season.

News of Carol Ann's death was reported throughout the United States, having been distributed by the Associated Press (AP). It also reported on accounts that the Pomranky family moved out of their forest home the day after the incident. The *Milwaukee Journal* ran a story on Friday, July 9, coming out of the wire service in Sault Ste. Marie, Michigan, with the headline: "Family Moves Out of Forest—Killing of Girl by Bear Causes Ranger to Quit Job as Towerman":

Mrs. Arthur Pomranky, whose 3-year-old daughter was carried off Wednesday [earlier reports indicate the incident happened on Tuesday] *and killed by a black bear, prepared Friday to move with her husband and 5-year-old son from the forest home where the tragedy happened.*

Pomranky said that he had resigned his job as towerman with the federal forest service to get his wife and son, Allen, away from the home. The Pomrankys lived near the Mission Hill lookout tower in the Marquette National Forest, about 30 miles west of here.

Little remains around this remote area near Point Iroquois where Carol Ann lost her life. She was laid to rest at Pine Grove Cemetery in Sault Ste. Marie, Michigan.

The Point Iroquois Lighthouse was replaced by an automatic light in the channel off Gros Cap, Ontario, in 1962. In 1975, it was placed in

Three-year-old Carol Ann Pomranky was laid to rest in 1948 in Sault Ste. Marie after being attacked and killed by a bear on Mission Hill. Her spirit has been known to visit the grounds of the Point Iroquois Lighthouse. *Michelle Walk.*

the National Register of Historic Places. Today, the property is under the jurisdiction of the U.S. Department of Agriculture's U.S. Forest Service, and it serves as a museum from mid-May through early October. Visitors are even encouraged to climb the spiral staircase to the top of the sixty-five-foot tower. The lighthouse is closed from October to May, but the grounds remain open.

POINT IROQUOIS LIGHTHOUSE
12942 West Lakeshore Drive
Brimley, MI 49715

LAKE HURON

10

OLD PRESQUE ISLE LIGHTHOUSE

N oted as one of the oldest lights on Lake Huron, the Old Presque Isle Lighthouse was built in 1840 at the southeast end of a peninsula about twenty-four miles north of Alpena.

Henry Woolsey was named the first keeper of this light, serving about seven years before he died. George Murray was the next tender, followed by Stephen Thorton, who took office on May 22, 1848, and resigned on July 27, 1853. Louis Metivier then managed the light until 1861, with Patrick Garrity (sometimes spelled Garraty) appointed as the final keeper until the light was decommissioned on June 1, 1871. The Garritys were well known, and tending lights was a family affair, with the father, mother, their four sons and two of their three daughters all serving in some capacity.

The Old Presque Isle Light's life was short, operating for a little more than three decades before it began to deteriorate. Instead of repairing the structure, the Lighthouse Board decided to use the appropriated funds to construct a pair of range lights (put into operation in 1870) and new light at the north end of the peninsula (opened in 1871). Today, all four lights remain standing as a testament to their maritime heritage and are popular sites for travelers to visit.

Sadly, over the years, the vacated light continued to be subjected to the harsh elements of time. A detailed account of the light's history has been documented on TerryPepper.com:

> *With the old light now obsolete, the station's lens and lantern were removed from the tower and shipped to the Detroit depot for use elsewhere. With the*

removal of the lantern, the tower was left uncapped and the windows and doors to the structures boarded-up to stand empty and decaying for 26 years until 1897 when the lighthouse reservation and structures were finally sold at public auction to Edward O. Avery of Alpena.

In the early 1900s, hotelier and Lansing milliner Bliss Stebbins (brother of A.C. Stebbins of the Lansing Wheelbarrow Company and one of eight original founders of the Oldsmobile company with R.E. Olds) purchased the lighthouse and its property at a tax sale for a mere seventy dollars. He had intended to use the grounds as a private park and picnic area for patrons of his nearby Grand Lake Hotel. His plans never developed, and he did nothing to preserve the historic lighthouse. By 1930, the walls were crumbling, the roof had collapsed and vandals were walking away with pieces of the structure as souvenirs. The account on TerryPepper.com continues:

Bliss's brother, Francis B. Stebbins, purchased the property in 1930, planning to rebuild the dwelling as a summer cottage for his family, however finding the structure to be unsalvageable he came to the same decision as the District Inspector some 70 years previous, deciding to demolish the structure and start anew. After dynamiting the crumbling walls, Stebbins finished work in 1939, with the structure built in a style reminiscent of an old English cottage.

Just ten years later, Francis purchased a larger summer home nearby and maintained the cottage as a guest house.

By the middle of the twentieth century, tourists began visiting the remote lighthouse grounds in greater numbers, and many were asking for tours of the tower and the home. Recognizing an opportunity, Francis began converting the property into a museum.

In 1961, he purchased a fourth-order Fresnel lens believed to have been originally at the South Fox Island Lighthouse on Lake Michigan and had it installed in the tower. He also commissioned a local man, Fred May, to reconstruct the lantern room atop the thirty-eight-foot tower. Francis also outfitted the cottage with period furnishings and maritime artifacts to complete the museum transformation.

Due to his tireless dedication, the Old Presque Isle Lighthouse was added to the Michigan Register of Historic Places on November 14, 1964, with the official marker dedication on June 19, 1965 (it was also placed in the National Register of Historic Places on April 11, 1973).

The ghost of former civilian caretaker George Parris has been seen on countless occasions at Old Presque Isle Lighthouse since he passed away in 1992. His spirit is credited with ongoing activity there over the last twenty-five-plus years. *Lorraine Parris.*

In 1965, when electricity was finally available, Francis set out to reactivate the light in the tower, but the Coast Guard had other thoughts on the matter. Permission to illuminate the light as a private navigational aid was denied, and the mechanism inside the tower was removed.

When Francis passed away in 1969, his son Jim inherited the complex and maintained it as a museum, hiring area high school and college girls as tour guides. In doing so, he attracted more young men than actual tourists, so in 1972, he hired George and Lorraine Parris as live-in caretakers. The retired couple took to their lighthouse duties immediately and with passion, welcoming visitors for more than twenty years. Even after George passed away in January 1992 of a heart attack, Lorraine continued to serve at the lighthouse they had called home. It was shortly after George's death that Lorraine first experienced an encounter she attributes to the ghost of her husband.

As the story goes, Lorraine was driving home one evening when she noticed a distinct glow coming from the point where the lighthouse stood. Knowing full well that there was no electricity running to the tower, she couldn't explain what she was seeing. It happened repeatedly not only to her but to others traveling both on the mainland and out in the fresh waters of Lake Huron.

The ghost light eventually became a matter of concern for mariners, because they weren't expecting to see a light at this location, and a rogue light could throw them off course. It took some time before Lorraine finally admitted what she saw, telling the Coast Guardsmen about it when they stopped by once for a visit. She told the servicemen she believed George was responsible.

Many a Guardsman was known to hang out with George in the tower after 1992. In fact, Lorraine said she would often pour the men—who would stop by regularly to check on her—a shot of whiskey along with one for her husband. The men would retreat to the top of the tower, where they'd toast

107

the one-time keeper, leaving his shot glass on the ledge. Later that night or the next evening, Lorraine would retrieve her husband's empty glass.

A more riveting story is set on a dark and stormy night when Lorraine was attempting to leave the cottage at the end of the tour day. As she reached for the handle of the door, she found it stuck as if someone was holding it shut from the outside. About that time, a large crack of lightning and rumble of thunder shook the cottage. Figuring it was best to ride out the storm, Lorraine sat back down and waited. When it had passed, she returned to the door and it opened with ease. As she walked to her car, she looked down and noticed a large circle of singed grass where lightning had struck. Had she been outside the cottage at the time, it was likely Lorraine would have been electrocuted.

To this day, she knows her beloved George was there that night looking after her.

A story by Rachel L. Jones published in the *Chicago Tribune* on September 23, 1994, under the headline "Lighthouse Passion Guides Georgianna Conte" shares a unique story about the then-thirty-nine-year-old registered nurse from Monroe, Michigan, who felt an undeniable connection to lighthouses.

While the article states "she can't say if she was a lighthouse keeper, or a lighthouse keeper's wife or child in a past life," the woman notes that in small ways, beacons have slowly been making their way into her life—through drawings, paintings, etchings and other artwork that she'd been purchasing over the years. "There's just this sense that they're almost calling me."

In August of that year, Georgianna traveled to the Old Presque Isle Lighthouse, where she nearly had the run of the place to wait for the ghost of George Parris. While there, she toured the home where Lorraine still lived, admiring her pictures and collections. She climbed the forty-five steps to the top of the tower.

"You can't see the ghost light from the lighthouse grounds," Lorraine said in the article. "You have to be across the bay, on a pier near the boat landing. At first the fuzzy white orb is so dim you think it is fog, but then, at a precise spot on the pier, it becomes distinct."

It was here that Georgianna saw the light for herself, at first thinking it was a reflection from the floodlights bouncing off the lens of the light or the glass that encased it. Yet, just moments later, at 9:15 p.m., Lorraine turned on the bright floodlights, which caused the ghost light to disappear while also dispelling Georgianna's theory.

"In my head, I need to believe that there needs to be some explanation for it," said Georgianna. "But in my heart, I want to believe it was George."

On Halloween 2014, Tom Kramer from UpNorthLive.com (WBPN TV 7/4) broadcast a story about the lighthouse, sharing both a widely known ghost story about Parris and hints as to a second resident spirit.

"We've also heard the caretaker also will talk to some of the children and no one else will see him. He's always kind, he doesn't scare the children or anything," said Jeni Matuszak, Presque Isle Township historian, referring to Parris and his encounters with others in the tower.

As to the illumination of the light, "It just gives a warm glow and everyone is excited when it comes on. There is no electricity hooked up and the Coast Guard has investigated it as to why it comes on because ships have seen it as well and there's no explanation," Matuszak said.

Medium Tammy Schuster was also interviewed during the segment, climbing the tower with Matuszak, where she revealed some new information about the spirits at the lighthouse.

"The face in the light is not his face because he looks different than that picture," Tammy said, referring to photographs taken by visitors that show a light reflection of a man in the giant fourth-order Fresnel lens. "That's the one in the light, that's the other gentleman from the older era that would be there," she noted as she flipped through an album in the museum—landing on an image of a man named Don S. Olds, a Stebbins family friend who wrote a poem about the light in 1936.

When asked more recently about that day at the light, Tammy said, "The thing I remember most was seeing a guy up in the lighthouse that I described vividly to them. Then we went down to the museum and looked through their photos and found him. He actually had written a song about the lighthouse. He definitely loves it there."

In the fall of 2017, Corey Atkins of *9/10 News* out of northern Michigan interviewed lighthouse docent Sally Dick about the ghostly activity at the light:

"Shortly after he died, his wife Lorraine was coming back from an errand and she looked up at the lighthouse because it was getting dark out and she saw the lighthouse come on, and she was like 'what is going on? How can I be seeing this light when there is no power?'" explained Sally.

The power to the light had been cut off for decades, so Lorraine kept the phenomenon to herself. But for three weeks the light kept appearing. That's when she called the Coast Guard to make sure no one reconnected the power.

'And they said, 'Lorraine, we hate to tell you this but there's no way light can come on out there. What do you think's going on?' and she said, 'Well,

In 1936, Don S. Olds wrote a poem about the Old Presque Isle Lighthouse, and in recent years, a local medium says she's seen his ghost in the giant lens at the top of the thirty-eight-foot tower. *Presque Isle Lighthouse Museum.*

Listed in both the Michigan and National Registers of Historic Places, the Old Presque Isle Lighthouse is one of four beacons in this community. *Author's Collection.*

you know what? It has to be my husband, George. He has come back to tell me he is still watching over me,' and to this day people still see the light go on. I have seen it," said Sally.

Men on freighters, fishermen all have seen the light that shouldn't be shining.

"You know they're telling the truth because fishermen and guys on the freighters aren't going to come in and tell me that story. They'll tell me a true story that they saw the light," explained Sally.

Even though this may be a little spooky, it seems George has a gentle soul. One time a little girl climbed the light tower by herself. When she came back down..."Her mom said, 'What's so funny?' and she said, 'Well, I was talking to the lighthouse keeper up there in the lighthouse,' and she said, 'There's no lighthouse keeper.' And the little girl said, 'Yes there is, look up there!' And there was this picture up there of George Paris [sic] *on the mantle she said, 'There he is, he's the one that made me laugh,' "* explained Sally.

I have had the pleasure of meeting Lorraine on two occasions over the years, but unfortunately I have yet to make George's acquaintance. In 2015, I presented "Michigan's Ghostly Beacons" on the lawn at dusk as part of the lighthouse's 175th anniversary celebration. Lorraine (along with her daughter, Alice) sat in the front row, as if she was about to critique my program and the stories I was about to share.

At the onset, I acknowledged her and briefly reminisced about when we met at the Great Lakes Lighthouse Festival in Alpena years before, when I presented a couple of sessions and she was the guest of honor. We sat together at dinner that night, and she shared detailed accounts with me about the ghost of her husband, George—stories I still tell today (and reinforced by accounts noted above), including of that summer night outside the Old Presque Isle Lighthouse. I remember saying something at the onset of my program like "I hope I get these stories right, if not, please correct me," to which she replied with a smirk, "I definitely will." At the end of the night, she added a bit more color to some of the stories, but I felt quite pleased that I had relayed them fairly accurately (at least to Lorraine's satisfaction).

By the mid-1990s, increasing costs for insurance and taxes forced Jim Stebbins to sell the property to the State of Michigan. In 1995, with funding provided by the Michigan Natural Resources Trust Fund and several private donors, the property was purchased by Presque Isle Township for use as a park and museum. The Old Presque Isle Lighthouse (along with the New Presque Isle Lighthouse up the road) is open for public tours from May through October.

OLD PRESQUE ISLE LIGHTHOUSE
5295 East Grand Lake Road
Presque Isle, MI 49777

11

SAGINAW RIVER REAR RANGE LIGHT, BAY CITY

H earing heavy footsteps on the spiral steel staircase of a lighthouse tower doesn't seem like something to be afraid of—unless the light in question has been vacant for more than forty years. Such is the case of the Saginaw River Rear Range Light in Bay City, built in 1876 and deactivated in 1960.

On his popular website LostInMichigan.net, photographer Mike Sonneberg from Saginaw (see cover photograph) states, "While I was researching the history of the old lighthouse, I came across some interesting stories of the old lighthouse being haunted. [A] serviceman stationed there claimed to have heard footsteps inside the old lighthouse even though he was the only one there and all the doors were locked."

The real question, of course, is who do those footsteps belong to? As with most lights, the culprit can often be identified as one (or more) of the former keepers.

Located about 220 miles northwest of Detroit along the Lake Huron coastline, Saginaw Bay saw its first settlers arrive in the 1830s. The lumber industry was taking shape here just as it was at other locations around the state of Michigan. Timber from the thumb area was shipped down the Saginaw River to the Saginaw Bay, where it would travel south through the Great Lakes to New York's Erie Canal and Hudson River to the East Coast.

Construction began on the first Saginaw Bay Lighthouse in the summer of 1839, and the project was completed and the light first illuminated in the fall of 1841. The sixty-two-foot-tall circular stone tower and one-and-a-half-story dwelling served this port town for about twenty-five years.

Peter Brawn (sometimes spelled Brown or Braun) was the eighth keeper at the Saginaw Bay Light, moving into the residence in March 1866 with his wife, Julia (also known as Juliann Tobey or Toby), and the youngest of their five children, sixteen-year-old son DeWitt Clinton "D.C." Brawn.

It is said that shortly after his appointment, Peter fell ill and was mostly bedridden. During his incapacitation, Julia tended the light with diligence, even though she wasn't recognized by the Lighthouse Service as an active keeper. DeWitt was known to assist his mother with the duties, also in an unofficial capacity.

Peter Brawn was the eighth keeper at the Saginaw Bay Light, moving into the original residence in March 1866 with his wife, Julia, and their youngest child, sixteen-year-old son DeWitt. *Bay County Historical Society.*

The following year, an increase in industrial operations and river traffic warranted a deeper waterway to accommodate larger ships, so the U.S. Army Corps of Engineers dredged the river. This made the lighthouse and the responsibilities of the Brawn family even more important. The region was growing up around them, and they were an integral part of the commercial development of the area. Peter passed away on March 18, 1873, at the age of sixty-three, at which time Julia was named the official keeper of record.

The original Saginaw lighthouse was replaced by what is considered the first range light system in Michigan in 1876. *The Lighthouse Encyclopedia: The Definitive Reference*, by Ray Jones (2004), credits DeWitt with developing the concept for range lights:

> *As a teenager, Brawn spent a lot of time on the water, and he noticed how the perspective of two objects changed as he floated past them. Brawn's insight was given a pratical application with the construction of the Saginaw River Range Lights in 1876. Its rear range tower stood 61 feet high and a considerable distance from a modest front range tower down on the riverbank. Functioning in tandem, the two beacons helped pilots steer a straight course through the river's channel.*

Range lights operate when two fixed lights are constructed a set distance apart so that vessels traveling on the correct course can line them up vertically

Julia Tobey Brawn Way outlived two husband keepers—Peter Brawn and George Way—during her years of tending the lights in Saginaw. *Bay County Historical Society.*

and follow them safely into port during nighttime. The light closer to the water, from the perspective of the ship traveling into shore, is considered the front range light, while the farther light is called the rear range light.

The Saginaw Front Range Light was located on the west bank of the Saginaw River, while the Rear Range Light—with its keeper's quarters—was constructed south of the river mouth, where it remains standing today. The range light concept was soon put in place by the Lighthouse Board at several sites on the Great Lakes and was later adopted throughout the service.

About this same time, in 1876 or 1877 depending on the source, Julia married a man thirteen years her junior. George Nelson Way was born March 3, 1829, in Canada, and according to an 1883 copy of *History of Bay County, Michigan*, "his early life [was] spent on the ocean, first as hand before the mast. He was afterward captain of a vessel on the lake." George's first wife, a Miss Wright, died in 1874; the couple had one daughter, Sarah Frances, born in 1858.

Upon their marriage, George moved into the lighthouse with Julia, and within a short period of time, she was demoted from her position as head keeper to first assistant. George was subsequently named acting keeper effective November 9, 1877. By the following spring, the "acting" had been removed from his title, and he officially took full charge of the lighthouse on June 6, 1878.

For the next several years, it was business as usual for the Ways until Julia found herself without a job altogether. On October 1, 1882, the first assistant position was abolished, leaving only George working at the light in an official capacity.

The next spring brought another interesting turn of events when the first assistant position was reinstated as an "acting" position in late May and assigned to Leonidus B. Charlton—who is referred to in the *History of Bay County, Michigan* as Julia Way's grandson. The appointment became official about three weeks later. This must have not sat well with Julia, who remained unemployed but living with her keeper husband at the light.

This new hierarchy was short lived, as George died at the light that October of asthma at the age of fifty-four. With that, Julia's life at her beloved lighthouse came to an end. Even Leonidus left his position, officially resigning six months into his service on November 23, 1883.

Only two keepers died during their lighthouse service in Saginaw: Peter Brawn (who served at the original light) in 1873 and George Way (who tended the range light) in 1883, and both were married to Julia at the time of their deaths. Was she simply unlucky in love? Or were they? Is it possible she was a Victorian-era black widow? After 150 years, it is hard to tell, but you can't help but wonder.

Little is known about Julia's life after her seventeen-plus years in lighthouse service. She passed away at the age of seventy-three on September 6, 1889, and is buried in Oak Ridge Cemetery in Bay City, Michigan. An article published the following day in the *Bay City Evening Press and Advocate* sheds light on a dedicated, noble and religious woman regarded as a leader in her community under the headline "Old Pioneer Gone—Sketch of the Life of Mrs. George N. Way":

The announcement of the death of Mrs. George N. Way (Mrs. Peter Brawn) was made in Thursday's issue of The Press. She was an old pioneer of Bay City and leaves a large circle of friends to mourn her death.

Deceased was born February 10, 1816, in Hellowell, Maine, her maiden name being Julia R. Toby. In 1831 she was married to Peter Brawn, and in 1845 removed to Mapleton, Ont. They came to Bay City a few years afterward and in 1864 Mr. Brawn was appointed by the government as lighthouse keeper, which office he held with honor until his death, which occurred January 24, 1872 [death records with Bay County note his death was on March 18, 1873]. *Dewitt C. Brawn, who still resides in this city, remained five years with his mother, attending to the lighthouse. Mrs. Brawn was remarried in 1877 to George N. Way. They lived at the lighthouse and continued to attend to the business for a period of five or six years more, when Mr. Way expired suddenly, leaving his widow entirely alone. She moved at once to their home, Pine Grove Place, situated on the north bank of Kawkawlin river, about four miles northwest of this city, being left in very good circumstances. The angel of death crossed her threshold at 7 o'clock Wednesday evening, ending a useful and Christian life. She was 73 years of age and leaves three sons and three daughters, as follows: Mrs. George Durfee, Bay City; Mrs. Westpointer, Lansing; Mrs. George*

Sproni, Pinconning; Arthur and DeWitt C., Bay City, and Benjamin, who lives in New York state. The latter will be unable to attend the funeral, which occurs from deceased's house on Sunday at 2 p.m., owing to sickness in his family.

Mrs. Way was a lady who possessed noble traits of character, being ever ready to aid the distressed and care for the needy. As she lived, so she died, a loving wife, a kind mother and a Christian woman. She will be remembered long by a wide acquaintance of dear friends as one of the noblest of earth. The remains will be interred in Oak Ridge cemetery in West Bay City.

The following spring, in 1890, DeWitt was awarded the contract to attend to the buoys in the Saginaw River, carrying on his family's legacy. According to a May 14, 1890 article in the *Bay City Evening Press*:

D.C. Brawn has received notice from Washington that his bid for attending the buoys at the mouth of the Saginaw river has been accepted and the contract awarded to him. The work has been done by Mr. Brawn the greater part of the past fifteen years, and his efficiency, no doubt, went far towards securing him the job. The range lights were just brought into use by Mr. Brawn at the mouth of the river, he having done the work himself and received his pay from subscriptions of the vessel men. When the new channel was dredged out he performed the same work and the lights gave excellent satisfaction. Subsequently the government put in permanent ranges and the old ones were discarded. Peter Brawn, father of D.C. Brawn, was lighthouse keeper for eight years at the above point, and when he died his widow continued ten years with the assistance of her son.

DeWitt passed away in 1931 at the age of eighty of chronic prostatitis and is buried in Elm Lawn Cemetery in Bay City, Michigan. According to *Legendary Locals of Bay City, Michigan*, by Ron Bloomfield:

Brawn remained actively identified with shipping throughout his life. He worked for a few years in the tug office of W.H. Sharp and in 1897 took the position of deputy clerk of customs for the port of Bay City. His service with the US Customs Office gained him the friendship of practically every captain and boatman entering the Saginaw River. During his more than a quarter century of government service, the duties collected through his office amounted to well over a million dollars.

As time passed, more than a dozen other men and women tended the Saginaw lighthouse. George Schinderette was the last official keeper, serving until 1939, at which time the lighthouse was transferred to the U.S. Coast Guard. For the next couple of decades, Guardsmen served as tenders of the light until it was extinguished in 1960. It then became a residence for the Coast Guard until its facilities were moved across the river.

In April 2013, Dave Rogers published a spirited tale on MyBayCity. com told to him by Don Comtois, a member of the Saginaw River Marine Historical Society, who heard the story from a former Coast Guardsman stationed at the light in 1980:

> *At the changing of the guard one dark night, the sailor hit the sack, only to be awakened by his relief man, a young salt who said he had heard something in the tower, going up and down the steps. Checking all the doors, they were found to be securely padlocked. But the noise persisted, and an eerie glow came from one side of the tower even though the moon shone on the other side.* [Comtois] *said the incident should be written up and sent to district headquarters in Detroit. "No way," the savvy older man said. "The last thing I want is to be called on the carpet before a bunch of officers in Detroit asking about a ghost!" Comtois said he tried to contact the Coast Guardsman after he left here, but mail was returned from his parents' home on Cape Cod "unable to forward." He later learned the man had entered a monastery in Spain and he has been unable to contact him.*

In August 2018, I traveled to Bay City to find the graves and death records for Peter, George, Julia and DeWitt as ongoing research for this book. I was in the Local History Room of the Alice & Jack Wirt Public Library (across from the Bay County Building downtown) asking the volunteer genealogists onsite to help me locate documents. A gentleman doing his own research overheard my questions, and he engaged in conversation, talking about the light, its keepers, the restoration and such. He said he was a member of the Saginaw River Marine Historical Society.

I mentioned that I had met some members of this group years before when I spoke at the Great Lakes Lighthouse Festival in Alpena. He asked if I had ever been to the lighthouse, and I admitted I had not. He offered a tour at a later date, and I gladly accepted. I told him I was off to the county clerk's office to look through the death logs before heading to Oak Ridge Cemetery to find Julia's grave—along with (hopefully) those of her husbands (earlier in the day I had visited DeWitt's burial site at Elm Lawn Cemetery

Julia Tobey Brawn Way is buried at the Oak Ridge Cemetery just outside of downtown Saginaw. Her husband Peter is buried to her left, and her marker is engraved with her husband George's name on the right side. *Author's Collection.*

on the other side of town). He offered to show me where the graves were, since I was unable to reach the sexton for the actual plot numbers and the cemetery is quite large. Again, I accepted his invitation of help.

I followed him a few miles from downtown to the cemetery, along the narrow drive to Julia's aging six-foot-tall marker. George's name was engraved on the right side of the stone, although no records indicated he was interred in the same site and he died six years before she did. Beside her, to the left, Peter's barely legible tombstone was on the ground, partially buried, after falling over many years before. My guide told me they were trying to raise the funds to restore the markers as part of the lighthouse's history.

I asked my guide what he knew about the deaths of Peter and George, if he knew any ghost stories, who did he think the ghosts were—the husbands? I shared with him my ongoing theory about Julia having a role in their deaths, even though I have no proof to substantiate my claim. It was just weird to me that she had two husbands die while in service at the light, ten years apart—while she lived with them. He didn't seem to buy my theory, which is probably a good thing.

He also said he thought perhaps it was Julia's spirit that still roamed the lighthouse, a lonely widow times two forever saddened by her losses. He admitted he'd never had a ghostly encounter before, but he'd heard stories from others. He then told me the same story noted above from 2013 on MyBayCity.com. It turns out this man who took the better part of the afternoon to assist me in my research was none other than Don Comtois, the man whose story I had already planned to include in this chapter. Coincidence? Perhaps, or maybe it was just one of those encounters that was meant to be.

In 1986, the Dow Chemical Company—the world's second-largest chemical producer, founded in 1897—purchased the facility and boarded it up. Although the light and its surrounding grounds are now private property and trespassing is prohibited, the nonprofit Saginaw River Marine Historical Society occasionally is granted access to the site for the purposes of historic research.

Founded in 1989 by a group of dedicated individuals interested in preserving the rich maritime heritage of the Saginaw River valley and Saginaw Bay, the Saginaw River Marine Historical Society is dedicated to the preservation and appreciation of the history of the Saginaw River and connecting waters. Public tours are offered on a very limited basis.

12

POINTE AUX BARQUES LIGHTHOUSE, PORT HOPE

No one knew more tragedy at Pointe aux Barques Lighthouse than Catherine (Doyle) Shook, wife of the first keeper, Peter, and mother to their eight children.

The Shooks came to the shores of Lake Huron, twelve miles south of Port Austin and six miles north of Port Hope, in 1848, and some say Catherine has never really left. Her ghost, dressed either in a full-length white gown or in all black as if she is in mourning, has been seen on countless occasions within the 1857 keeper's residence and around the grounds.

Tourists and museum volunteers have also reported seeing a woman wearing an apron appearing in the second-floor window, hearing footsteps in the tower, smelling wafts of pipe tobacco and feeling icy spots brush past them within the historic home. Local paranormal groups have recorded activity they suspect belongs to Catherine.

The French name Pointe aux Barques translates to "Point of Small Boats"—the waters here are very shallow, and only small boats could safely navigate into port. In 1847, President James Polk allocated $5,000 to construct the light nearly five miles east-southeast of the actual Pointe aux Barques, at the extreme northwest tip of the thumb. The keeper's residence and twenty-eight-foot detached tower sat on three acres and were cobbled together using stones taken from the lakeshore.

Peter Loren Shook (originally spelled Schuck before the name was Americanized, also sometimes printed as Schook) was born in New York State in 1808 and was nearly forty when he took on the role of tending the newly constructed lighthouse on March 6, 1848.

A year or so into his service, Peter suffered a terrible fate on the waters of Lake Huron, and he was lost at sea forever. Different versions of what happened to him that spring have been reported, but because no body was ever recovered, no official cause of death is on record.

The Pointe aux Barques Lighthouse Society states on its website that on that fateful day, Catherine fell ill, and Peter went in search of Dr. John S. Heath to tend to his beloved wife. Afterward, the doctor enjoyed supper alongside the family, and with a storm looming in the distance, he was invited to spend the night at the light.

He declined, as he had other patients to see early the next day, and the doctor and Peter set out by boat (as it was easier and quicker than traveling through the dense woods, given that the only roads at the time were rugged Native American trails) back to town. The storm had blown in, and the waves were soon tossing the small boat around until the two men were thrown into the water, where they both drowned.

A newspaper article published in New York's *Buffalo Daily Republic* on Monday, April 23, 1849 (and later reprinted in the *Buffalo Weekly Republic* on Tuesday, May 1 of that year), tells the story under the headline "Dr. Heath Drowned":

> *We learn, says the* Detroit Bulletin *of the 19th inst., from a friend residing at Port Huron, that it is now rendered certain that Dr. John S. Heath, formerly of that village, has met a watery grave. The boat in which he left his mills to come down to Port Huron, was found a day or two ago on the beach, ten or twelve miles above Lexington, where it had probably been washed ashore with one of the masts carried away. In company with Dr. H was two of his lumbermen, whose names we do not learn, and Capt. Peter Shook, the keeper of the Point Au Barque [sic] lighthouse, who was on his way to Detroit for supplies. Dr. Heath was an esteemed citizen, who had represented his county in the legislature, and had for a number of years been Sheriff of St. Clair county, and Deputy Collector of Customs at Port Huron.*

The news was printed by the *Milwaukee Daily Sentinel* on Monday, April 30, 1849, with a slightly different story under the headline "The Lake Huron Disaster":

> *The* Detroit Advertiser *has the following in regard to the late disaster on Lake Huron.*

The loss of Dr. John S. Heath and his son Henry, aged about 12 years, a hired man and Peter L. Shook, light house keeper at Point Aux Barque [sic], mentioned a few days since as a rumor, is fully confirmed. Dr. H's wife and the rest of his family were not on board. The above company left Point Aux Barque, in a small boat, on the 31ˢᵗ of March, for Port Huron, and all perished before reaching their destination.

The boat has been found, with holes cut thro' the bottom with a pocket knife, indicating that they were cut to enable the unfortunate passengers to cling to her after she capsized. Mr. Shook was on his way down after supplies for the light house.

In any case, Peter perished, and Catherine was left a widow. Not only was she distraught over the loss of her husband, but she was also left wondering where she would live and how she would afford to care for her large family. Thankfully, the U.S. Lighthouse Service offered her the position of lighthouse keeper at a rate of $350 a year, which seemed to solve most of her problems. She would remain in the home she had come to love, not have to uproot her children and was able to make a decent living. And in doing so, she became Michigan's first female lighthouse keeper.

But her misfortune was not over.

On June 11, 1849, a fire broke out in the small eight-hundred-square-foot keeper's dwelling that left Catherine with serious burns and forced her family out of the house. The next day, Henry B. Miller, superintendent and inspector of lights for the northwest lakes, stopped by to investigate the situation and filed a formal report to his superiors:

I regret to announce to you that in making this light today about 10 o'clock a.m. we found the dwelling belonging to it destroyed by fire. I learned from Mrs. Shook the keeper that the fire was first discovered yesterday morning between 9 and 10 o'clock, and that all human efforts to arrest the flames proved unavailing. The fire as I learned from her was first discovered in the kitchen part of the building between the ceiling and roof. I made a through [sic] examination of the ruins and came to the following conclusions as to the origin of the fire. The chimney in this part of the building was constructed of rough flat stone, leaving large crevices in the wall, which were filled with mortar. Although a tight chimney when new, the action of the fire served to dry up and contract the mortar, leaving large opening in the wall through which sparks were forced by the wind and sat [sic] fire to the building where it was first discovered. I am strengthened in this belief from the fact that the family, instead of using the fireplace, used a cook stove, the pipe of which entered the chimney below the ceiling, and was safely secured so that the fire could not have caught from the stove pipe. What I learned and saw, I would exonerate the keeper from all blame, and ascribe the fire to a defect in the chimney. The circumstances of the fire is more to be regretted, as the husband of the keeper but lately found a watery grave in Lake Huron, and this affliction on this account falls with a double severity upon the widow who was lately appointed in his place. By this catastrophy [sic] the widow not only lost a considerable portion of her furniture, but was badly burned in her attempt to keep the fire from the main building. They have erected temporarily a small shanty, which is very uncomfortable and unhealthy. I hope therefore no time will be lost in having the dwelling rebuilt. I think the main walls are not sufficiently injured, but by a little repairing they will answer for a new dwelling. The keeper complained that the chimneys always smoked badly, rendering them often entirely unfit for use, and I would therefore recommend that in rebuilding the dwelling, the chimneys be made of brick, which would obviate this defect, and secure these in future more firmly against fire. The tower of the lighthouse also wants painting and whitewashing, which could perhaps be done the cheapest at the time of rebuilding the dwelling. I may add that the Light-house is well kept and that we discovered the light last night at a distance of some 15 miles. The keeper is the mother of 8 small children, and through her afflictions is worthy of our warmest sympathy and as I am convinced, that no blame can be ascribed to her in the building of the dwelling, I hope you will continue to entrust this light to her care.

Catherine went on to tend the Pointe aux Barques Lighthouse until resigning from service on March 19, 1851. She died nine years later on August 9, 1860, at the age of fifty. Her youngest child, Eugene, would have been about ten or twelve years old when she passed; her oldest son, Ignatius, was about thirty-one. Catherine is buried in Oakwood Cemetery in New Baltimore, Macomb County, where she shares a marker with Peter.

Given the loss of her husband and her own short life, it's no wonder that the ghost of Catherine Shook remains unsettled at this historic light.

John Robinson, an on-air personality for 99.1 WFMK in Lansing, has been sharing ghost stories from around Michigan for years on the station's website, 99wfmk.com. Under the headline "The Apparition of Pointe Aux Barques Lighthouse," he posted brief details about the female former keeper: "People have claimed to see the spirit of Catherine walking along the edge

Catherine Shook was just thirty-nine years old when her husband died at sea, leaving her, a widow with eight children, to tend the light. Although Peter's body was never recovered, his name was engraved on her headstone at Oakwood Cemetery in New Baltimore, Macomb County, when she passed in 1860. *Robert Yarrington.*

of the cliff, dressed in mourning clothes....She has also been spotted in the window of the second floor, wearing an apron," he wrote. "Along with an apparition being seen, footsteps ascending & descending the tower stairs and giggling has been heard, cold spots have been felt and burning tobacco has been smelled."

An account on the *Huron County View* website shared details about a 2010 weekend visit by the Southeast Michigan Paranormal Society, which is based out of Clinton Township:

> *"There is every reason to believe the lighthouse proper is haunted," Scott, the team leader reported. "As we were doing some evp (electronic voice phenomenon) work in the living room, we heard loud thuds coming from overhead. Climbing the stairs, the sounds of something scraping along the floor came from the same area. We found in the bedroom to the left of the staircase the rocking chair had moved about two feet and it was rocking." The team also recorded the sounds of giggling in that upstairs bedroom.*
>
> *"The spirit here…are constantly on the move. When we were downstairs, we heard heavy footsteps coming from upstairs. When we were upstairs we heard movements downstairs. We recorded heavy footsteps on the tower stairway and in the hallway. We will have a full written report of our findings for you, but for now, remember the spirits here are old spirits and will not harm you or your guests. They are just lost souls searching for eternity."*

When contacted recently about this account, the group was quick to respond:

> *We did investigate there for a weekend and had an incredible time. It's been years ago but there is definitely activity there. We were downstairs in the main house and heard something being moved across the floor....When we went upstairs to check…a child's rocking chair had moved into the closet. We also got many EVPs…a few so clear that when going over the audio I thought it was one of our investigators talking. We also had a lot of K-II hits especially in the upstairs bedroom where there was an organ....Whoever was up there didn't like us near the organ....When asked questions the K-II would red line but only when questions were asked.*

A K-II meter is one of the many devices used to help detect high-level electromagnetic field (EMF) emissions during a paranormal investigation.

Through a series of colored lights, the meter picks up on potential energy that might be attributed to unseen ghosts or spirits.

Jeff Shook, great-great-great-great-grandson of Catherine and Peter, has followed in his ancestors' footsteps as the current owner of the Port Sanilac Lighthouse, forty-five miles south along the Lake Huron shoreline in Michigan's thumb. Over the years, he's made countless visits to the Pointe aux Barques light and has been researching his family's historic ties to the area's maritime heritage. But he says he's never personally experienced any of the spirits that are said to still roam the grounds (nor, he said, has he had any encounters at the lighthouse he owns).

Despite reports from the paranormal society and accounts published online or in other books, Bill Bonner, the current president of the Point aux Barques Lighthouse Society, said via email that he does not believe the lighthouse or the area around it is haunted. "As a student of the paranormal in my younger days, I believe I would feel a spirit presence. None here."

The eighty-nine-foot-tall Pointe aux Barques Lighthouse tower is an active aid to navigation and is one of the oldest operating lights on the Great Lakes. Since 2002, the volunteers of the Pointe aux Barques Lighthouse Society have maintained a museum within the former keeper's residence. Both the museum and tower are open to the public from Memorial Day weekend through mid-October.

POINTE AUX BARQUES LIGHTHOUSE
7320 Lighthouse Road
Port Hope, MI 48468

13

FORT GRATIOT LIGHTHOUSE, PORT HURON

Michigan's oldest lighthouse (and the second built on the Great Lakes) predates the state's acceptance into the Union by a dozen years—the former dating to 1825 and the latter 1837. With nearly two hundred years of history, there are bound to be a number of ghosts that remain at this still-active lighthouse and its surrounding public beach and park. As many as five ghosts have been identified so far as part of recent paranormal investigations at the light—two former keepers, a Coast Guardsman, a young girl and a teenage boy.

The military outpost Fort Gratiot was the first establishment here in 1814. Designed by Lucius Lyon (who later became one of Michigan's first U.S. senators) and named after General Charles Gratiot, the fort guarded the intersection of Lake Huron and the St. Clair River in present-day Port Huron.

In 1823, Congress appropriated $3,500 for the construction of a light in the Michigan territory, and two years later, the original lighthouse was activated near where the first Blue Water Bridge stands.

Two temporary keepers were stationed at Fort Gratiot in those early years—Rufus Hatch, who died just forty-five days after being appointed, and Jean Desmayer, who served for only two months.

Colonel George McDougall was the first official keeper here, appointed on November 22, 1825, after speculation that he used his political influence to secure the position. From the onset, he noted concerns about the light. His reports indicate that the stairs were so steep that they had to be climbed sideways and that the door into the lantern room was barely large enough for a man to squeeze through (some reports note it measured eighteen inches by twenty-one and a quarter inches). McDougall was anything but a small man (reportedly weighing between 200 and 300 pounds), which may explain why he had difficulty accessing the top of the tower.

It was likely no surprise to McDougall that the poorly designed and hastily built light collapsed during a summer storm in 1828. A new light was constructed two years later north of the fort in a location that made it easier for ships to spot as they entered the rapids at the head of the St. Clair River. Originally just sixty-five feet tall, it was extended to its present height of eighty-two feet in the early 1860s.

A short biography on Colonel McDougall published on Michigan.gov under the Department of Military & Veteran Affairs noted:

> *He became a lawyer, but in addition to his legal practice he held various offices and engaged in diverse activities. He was a man of eccentric temperament, so much so that he seems to have been regarded by his contemporaries as somewhat abnormal mentally. In 1810, he was foreman of the grand jury which presented Governor Hull and Judges Witherell and Woodward for tyrannical conduct. At a subsequent date, he was disbarred by the judges for his conduct before them, and the probation was removed only after he had made a humble apology to the court. Notwithstanding his quarrelsome disposition, McDougall was popular with the French element of Detroit whose language he spoke as fluently as he spoke English. In his later years, prosperity forsook him and he obtained an appointment as lighthouse keeper at Fort Gratiot on the St. Clair River. This position he retained until his death, about the year 1840.*

With such a reputation, it's no wonder that Colonel McDougall—who died a bachelor on October 15, 1842, at the age of seventy-six—is one of the potential spirits at unrest at Fort Gratiot. The Motor Cities Ghost Hunters, who have hosted several public evening sessions, have encountered a former keeper on at least one occasion.

In the spring of 2012, the paranormal team visited the lighthouse and keeper's quarters where they documented the sounds of doors closing by themselves, footsteps in conjunction with the motion detectors going off, mumbling voices, cameras that unexplainably stopped working and one person who "sensed the presence of a lighthouse keeper."

On their website, MotorCityGhostHunters.com, a conclusion from that visit noted that "there appears to be energy in the complex of the lighthouse

Fort Gratiot Lighthouse, near Port Huron, is the first of Michigan's nearly 130 historic beacons, dating back to the 1820s. It is still an active navigational aid on southern Lake Huron. *Author's Collection.*

and the light keeper's house. However, it is possible that some of the energy can be attributed to residual energy based on the history of the area. On the other hand, several of the [audio evidence] responses that were captured, while faint, seem to be intelligent in their response."

The group returned to the lighthouse facility the following spring, where even more activity was documented: "Team 2 went into the living quarters and first went into the attic of the building where a Coast Guard officer allegedly hung himself. We had little activity but did experience movement through the laser grid and interaction through the Frank's Box."

According to Ghost-Tech.com, a "Frank's Box," "Spirit Box" or "Ghost Box" is a device created by Frank Sumption as a way to further his interest in EVP research. "Contacting spirits through the use of frequency devices or so-called boxes as a medium for direct communication has been a huge topic of discussion lately in the paranormal community."

It should be noted that no online record of a Guardsman's suicide could be found to substantiate this claim.

As part of the 2013 visit, the ghost hunters also reported prevalent flashlight activity in the basement living quarters and, through a series of questions, determined they were speaking to a former lighthouse keeper.

A third visit was recorded in late May 2014 that proved to be the most lucrative in terms of paranormal activity. Once again, the team heard footsteps and voices. They also reported seeing shadows moving back and forth in a large area of the second floor and even had one team member's water bottle tip over from where it was sitting on the windowsill.

During this visit, the ghost hunters reveal names of spirits they've encountered: "John began the session by trying to communicate with a spirit named Bob, who was one of the lighthouse keepers we have previously communicated with."

Could this be Robert H. "Lighthouse Bob" Hanford, a civilian who played the role of keeper until just prior to his 2010 death? A review of the list of keepers from Fort Gratiot Light, compiled by Phyllis L. Tag of the Great Lakes Lighthouse Research and published on TerryPepper.com, shows no other keepers between 1825 and 1950 by the name of Robert or Bob.

Hanford was noted as one of the biggest supporters of the Fort Gratiot Lighthouse, where he led thousands of people through tours over a twenty-year period. A detailed account of his life on FindAGrave.com states that he was a member of the U.S. Coast Guard Auxiliary and assumed duties as lighthouse keeper here in 1988:

> *He looked the part of a lightkeeper....Dressed in a period-correct U.S. Lighthouse Service uniform, Bob would proudly share the history of the station's construction and service life as a major aid to navigation, as well as stories and artifacts from the site and the keepers who preceded him. He was rightfully proud of his visitor logs, which contained thousands of names and hometowns of the guests who had come to visit him and his beloved lighthouse from all over the United States and the world.*

The only keeper to serve longer than "Lighthouse Bob" was Frank Kimball, who came to Fort Gratiot on October 31, 1894, after serving twelve years farther up the shore at the Port Austin Reef Light.

In an article published in the *Herald Times* out of Port Huron, Michigan, on July 8, 1927, Kimball was quoted as saying, "Yes, I like the service. It is interesting if you grow up with it as I have. You stay a good many years, perhaps because you're foolish. But it's fascinating and after all, it is part of a great system of service."

Left: Robert H. "Lighthouse Bob" Hanford, a civilian who played the role of keeper for nearly twenty years until just prior to his 2010 death, is one of the many ghosts at the Fort Gratiot Lighthouse. *Port Huron Museum.*

Right: Appointed in 1894 and retiring in 1929, Frank Kimball is noted as the longest-serving keeper at Fort Gratiot, dedicating thirty-three years here and forty-five years overall on Lake Huron. His spirit remains active at the light to this day. *Port Huron Museum.*

Kimball retired in September 1929 after serving thirty-three years at Fort Gratiot and dedicating forty-five years overall to the lighthouse service in Michigan. He died of cancer at the age of seventy-four on December 28, 1933, and he is buried at Forest Lawn Cemetery in Saginaw.

During the 2014 visit, the ghost hunters also encountered this keeper's ghost.

"Team 3 began their investigation inside the Coast Guard duplex," they noted on their website. "They tried to make contact using the spirit box. They heard the name 'Kimball' come through. When asked if they are unhappy that we are here with them, the spirit box stated 'I am.' "

The final session in the duplex featured the entire team together, with four of the men in the basement attempting to communicate with Kimball.

"Guy had a very personal experience the last time he investigated with the team in 2013. [He] said he felt a presence while in the basement. After stating this, he said he felt better and a sense of calm was felt by all in the basement."

Two other spirits believed to be within the Fort Gratiot grounds are a young girl by the name of Sarah and a thirteen-year-old boy named Josh, who is believed to have drowned in the lake or river nearby in 2013. However, a search of Newspapers.com found no accounts of any accidents that would be tied to these two ghosts.

Those looking to try ghost hunting firsthand are invited to take part in one of the annual investigations held in October with the Motor City Ghost Hunters. Available only to those over the age of eighteen, the five-hour event takes participants inside the tower and duplex and around the grounds in search of spirits. There is even an option for a limited number of people to spend the night in the duplex on the property from midnight until 9:00 a.m.

Public tours of Fort Gratiot, including tower climbs (weather permitting), are offered from early May through December, although early- and late-season dates are limited to the weekends. Tours are available on a first come, first served basis.

FORT GRATIOT LIGHTHOUSE
2802 Omar Street
Port Huron, MI 48060

RESOURCES

Great Lakes Lighthouse Keepers Association
www.gllka.com

Historical Society of Michigan
www.hsmichigan.org

Library of Congress
www.loc.gov

Library of Michigan
www.michigan.gov/libraryofmichigan

Michigan Historical Center
www.seekingmichigan.org

National Archives
www.archives.gov

Promote Michigan
www.promotemichigan.com

Pure Michigan
www.michigan.org

Seeing the Light: Lighthouses of the Western Great Lakes
www.terrypepper.com

Travel Marquette
www.travelmarquettemichigan.com

Upper Peninsula Paranormal Research Society
www.facebook.com/UPPRSParanormal

Upper Peninsula Travel and Recreation Association
www.uptravel.com

U.S. Coast Guard
www.uscg.mil

West Michigan Tourist Association
www.wmta.org

Lake Michigan

1. South Haven Keeper's Dwelling

Historical Association of South Haven
www.southhavenlight.org

Michigan Maritime Museum
www.michiganmaritimemuseum.org

South Haven Area Chamber of Commerce
www.southhavenmi.com

South Haven VanBuren County Convention and Visitors Bureau
www.southhaven.org

2. White River Light Station, Whitehall

Sable Points Lighthouse Keepers Association
www.splka.org

White Lake Area Chamber of Commerce
www.whitelake.org

White Lake Area Historical Society
www.whitelakeareahistoricalsociety.com

3. South Manitou Island Lighthouse

Manitou Islands Memorial Society
www.manitouislandsmemorialsociety.org

Preserve Historic Sleeping Bear
www.phsb.org

Sleeping Bear Dunes National Lakeshore
www.nps.gov/slbe

Sleeping Bear Dunes Visitors Bureau
www.sleepingbeardunes.com

4. Waugoshance Shoal Lighthouse, Mackinaw City

Emmet County, Michigan
www.emmetcounty.org

Mackinaw Area Visitors Bureau
www.mackinawcity.com

Shepler's Mackinac Island Ferry
www.sheplersferry.com

Ugly Ann Boat Cruises
www.mackinawtour.com

5. *Seul Choix Point Lighthouse, Gulliver*

Keweenaw Video Productions
www.keweenawvideo.com

Manistique Tourism Council
www.visitmanistique.com

Seul Choix Point Lighthouse Park & Museums
www.greatlakelighthouse.com

LAKE SUPERIOR

6. *Big Bay Point Lighthouse*

The Inn at Big Bay Point Lighthouse Bed and Breakfast
www.bigbaylighthouse.com

Marquette Regional History Center
www.marquettehistory.org

7. *Marquette Harbor Lighthouse*

Marquette Maritime Museum
www.mqtmaritimemuseum.com

8. *Whitefish Point Lighthouse, Paradise*

Great Lakes Shipwreck Museum
www.shipwreckmuseum.com

Motor City Ghost Hunters
motorcityghosthunters.com

Paradise Area Tourism Council
www.michigansparadise.com

9. *Point Iroquois Lighthouse, Brimley*

Bay Mills–Brimley Historical Society
www.baymillsbrimleyhistory.org

Point Iroquois Lighthouse
www.fs.usda.gov/recarea/hiawatha/recarea/?recid=13342

LAKE HURON

10. *Old Presque Isle Lighthouse*

Alpena Area Convention & Visitors Bureau
www.visitalpena.com

The Lighthouses at Presque Isle, Michigan
www.presqueislelighthouses.org

Thunder Bay National Marine Sanctuary & Great Lake Maritime Heritage
Center
www.thunderbay.noaa.gov

11. *Saginaw River Rear Range Light, Bay City*

Bay County Historical Society
www.bchsmuseum.org

Great Lakes Bay Regional Convention & Visitors Bureau
www.gogreat.com

Saginaw River Marine Historical Society
www.saginawrivermhs.wixsite.com/srmhs

12. *Pointe aux Barques Lighthouse, Port Hope*

Huron County Historical Society
www.thehchs.org

Huron County Parks
www.huroncountyparks.com

Point aux Barques Lighthouse Society
www.pointeauxbarqueslighthouse.org

Thumb Area Tourism Council
www.thumbtourism.org

13. Fort Gratiot Lighthouse, Port Huron

Blue Water Area Convention & Visitor Bureau
www.bluewater.org

Port Huron Area History & Preservation Association
www.phahpa.org

Port Huron Museum & Fort Gratiot Lighthouse
www.phmuseum.org/fort-gratiot-lighthouse

AUTHOR'S NOTE

This manuscript is a compilation of historical dates and other information from a variety of sources and firsthand accounts. While details are not always consistent, what is printed here represents an honest attempt to relay the facts or accounts as shared with this author as best as possible. Theories are based on timelines for the given lighthouses and keepers and are noted as such. Also, given the topic of ghosts or spirits is subjective, stories may not be considered factual by all individuals. If you have a ghost story or photographs to share, please email Travel@PromoteMichigan.com.

ABOUT THE AUTHOR

Dianna Stampfler has been writing professionally since her junior year at Plainwell High School, when she was also a reporter for a local weekly newspaper. By her senior year, she had her own column in that paper, was serving as news editor of her award-winning school newspaper and was also working in the newsroom at a local radio station (following in the footsteps of her father, who has been a DJ for more than fifty-five years).

She graduated from Western Michigan University with a dual major in English with an emphasis in community journalism and communications with an emphasis in broadcasting. Dianna went on to work in public relations at Otsego Public Schools, where she also launched a middle school and elementary student newspaper program. Within four years, she was advising one of the top middle school papers in the state of Michigan until she was forced out following a highly publicized case involving First Amendment issues against her student journalists.

In 1997, Dianna began working in Michigan's tourism industry, promoting destinations within a forty-one-county region at the West Michigan Tourist Association. In 2004, she launched Promote Michigan, a public relations consulting company specializing in the hospitality, tourism, agriculture, culinary, natural resources, recreation, history and culture industries around her home state. It is her passion to share the stories of the people, places and products of Michigan.

Over the past twenty years, Dianna has penned countless articles for publications such as *Pure Michigan Travel Ideas*, *Michigan Blue* magazine, *Michigan Home & Lifestyle* magazine, *Women's Lifestyle*, *AAA Living*, *West Michigan Carefree Travel*, *Lake Michigan Circle Tour & Lighthouse Guide* and countless others, as well as contributing to various tourism-based blogs around Michigan (including her own at PromoteMichigan.com). She is also a regular guest on a variety of radio and television programs. *Michigan's Haunted Lighthouses* is her first (but hopefully not her last) book.

Dianna is the mother of two adult children, Mollie and Caleb; she currently resides in northwest Michigan.